The Drama of Decision

The Drama of Decision

Baptism in the New Testament

Oscar Stephenson Brooks

HENDRICKSON
PUBLISHERS
PEABODY, MASSACHUSETTS 01961-3473

For
Charlie Alston Brooks

and the memory of
Jessie Alyce Stephenson Brooks

TABLE OF CONTENTS

Preface

It is my persuasion that serious Bible study can be presented in a readable fashion. I have been serious about the study presented here, and you the reader will have a judgement upon its readability. The subject matter is the Christian practice of baptism. Innumerable books on this subject fill endless shelves in theological libraries; so one might ask, Why another book on the subject?

One reason a person writes is to satisfy personal interest. I have been mysteriously curious about the ritual of baptism ever since first I experienced it over a half-century ago, for in my spiritual pilgrimage I, like others, often reflected upon those primal experiences—wondering, What does it mean to me? as well as, How has it come to have such a meaning? Always Jesus' baptism by John was central in my thinking: What brought Jesus to John and what significance did the act of baptism have, or could have had for Jesus? Did Jesus administer baptism? Why did he command his disciples to practice it? How does this inform my reflection on the experience of baptism? In what way does baptism "put on Christ," or how is it associated with Christ's death? Of course, a serious study of a single paragraph in the New Testament might answer these questions adequately, but there is more.

Another reason a person writes is to meet a perceived need. In Christian circles is there a holistic statement about baptism, i.e., is there a statement that comprehends the multifaceted baptismal texts of the New Testament in such a way that a clear, succinct understanding of the ritual can be articulated? Baptism obviously means many things to many people. Usually the meaning has come through church, family, or cultural tradition. While each meaning may very well express some aspect of the biblical material, has it incorporated enough? There is always the need to reexamine, rethink, and rearticulate one's understanding of significant Christian doctrines. This is not to set aside former statements, but rather to bring clarity. I am convinced that students of the Bible have overlooked the possibility that there is a common theme running through the baptismal texts of the New Testament. I hope this can be demonstrated in the following pages.

My academic study of baptism began in graduate school when a part of my dissertation research involved the meaning of "water" in the Fourth Gospel. Later a specific study of "The Johannine Eucharist" (*Journal of Biblical Literature* 82 [1963]: 293–300) convinced me of the possibility of a similar theme for baptism and the supper. Additional studies in baptismal texts were done in "A Contextual Interpretation of Galatians 3:27" (*Studia Biblica 1978*, 3:47–56,) and "I Peter 3:21—The Clue to the Literary Structure of the Epistle" (*Novum Testamentum* 16 [1974]: 290–305). The study in 1 Peter persuaded me that the entire book is a baptismal tract and that the meaning of baptism in 1 Peter 3:21 is in harmony with other New Testament baptismal texts. Other studies indicate that there is a common meaning for baptism throughout the New Testament.

The title of this work capsulizes the thesis: baptism is the drama of decision. This must be elaborated. In the chapters ahead I have tried to show how each baptismal text fits into this thesis. While I am stating the thesis first, the reader must not immediately assume that the thesis interprets the text; rather I would urge that the texts give rise to the thesis. Throughout the study attention must be given to the substance of the decision.

The method employed here is not debate with other authors. I do not state another's position and then proceed to negate it. The proceedure is to interpret carefully each text at hand, making use of the appropriate tools of interpretation, using notes to indicate alternate points of view and technical matters. This permits a clear presentation to those wishing to maintain the flow of thought, and at the same time provides technical matters for those interested.

The text begins with a general description of the religious milieu of first-century Palestine and deals with John the Bapist's baptism, because its practice and its antecedents are crucial for understanding the remainder of the New Testament texts. Jesus' baptism in the Jordan River was important to the Gospel writers and thus demands our attention. Acts, John, and Paul receive special attention; and 1 Peter is an appropriate conclusion.

Although I must assume final responsibility for the substance of this study, it is appropriate to thank especially my wife, Sally, who has made this work easier for me by making the first typescript from the peculiar handwriting. Without her patient assistance this work would not be possible.

Abbreviations

AB	Anchor Bible
BAG	*A Greek-English Lexicon of the New Testament and Other Early Christian Literature*, Bauer, Arndt, and Gingrich (1957)
CD	Damascus Document or Zadokite Documents
IDB	*Interpreter's Dictionary of the Bible* 5 vols., ed. G. A. Buttrick et al. (1962–1976)
JBL	*Journal of Biblical Literature*
JTS	*Journal of Theological Studies*
LSJ	*A Greek-English Lexicon*, eds. Liddell & Scott, rev. Jones & McKenzie (1968)
M&M	*The Vocabulary of the Greek Testament*, Moulton and Milligan (1930; reprint 1980)
NTS	*New Testament Studies*
TDNT	*Theological Dictionary of the New Testament* 10 vols., eds. Kittel and Friedrich (1964–1976)
1QS	Community Rule, or Manual of Discipline

Baptism now saves you . . .
　　　as a declaration
　　　of an appropriate awareness
　　　toward God
　　　through the resurrection of Jesus Christ
1 Peter 3:21

1 | *The Urgency of Decision*

Whenever and wherever people are found, we are confronted with choices; decisions must be made. Many voices of society and its institutions vie for our response—voices of religious tones, voices of political and economic ideologies, voices offering status and prestige, or promising identification with an "in" group or an "out" group. In one way or another we all respond to these voices.

In the third decade of the first century A.D., a voice cried in the wilderness of Judea: "Repent for the kingdom of heaven is at hand." But this was not the only voice calling the people of that day to decision. It was only . . .

A Voice Among Voices

The temple in Jerusalem had stood as a symbol of religion and faith for almost a thousand years. Encouraged by Haggai and Zechariah, Zerubbabel rebuilt in 520 B.C. the Solomonic temple razed by the Babylonians. Herod the Great, ambitious for kingly prestige, sought to restore the temple to the glory of Solomon's original efforts. The project, undertaken around 20 or 19 B.C., soon completed the rebuilding of the temple itself, but all the auxilliary structures were not completed until A.D. 63 or 64.

It is not always easy to imagine the impressive nature of the temple in the first century A.D. Located at the southeast corner of Jerusalem, its height was accentuated by the valleys that dropped off sharply to the south and east, and somewhat less to the west. The façade of the temple measured one-hundred-fifty feet wide and the center portion stood one-hundred-fifty feet tall with an entrance into the vestibule measuring thirty-seven and one-half by one-hundred-five feet. Beyond this opening could be viewed the massive doors standing eighty-two and one-half feet high. The exterior of the temple was constructed of white stone; and according to the Jewish historian Josephus, the entire façade was overlaid with gold. So brilliant was the reflection of the sun that one could hardly look at the building from certain angles.[1]

What an expression of religious devotion! But this was not all. The temple did not stand as a monument; it served as a place where devotion to God was continually displayed. A daily ritual was well formulated from the priestly interpretation of the laws. Every day before dawn priests were up and busy in the temple area preparing for the daily ministrations. Having properly purified themselves, they proceeded to prepare the altar for the morning sacrifice. Pyres were lit for the twofold purpose of consuming the portions left over from the day before, and to prepare for the new sacrifice. Priests selected by lot slaughtered and prepared the sacrificial animal whose blood was sprinkled on the corners of the altar. Following the rite of sacrifice incense was burned. Sacrifices were offered both morning and evening, and special ceremonies honored the great festival days of the Jewish faith: Passover, the Feast of Weeks, civil New Year, Day of Atonement, and others.

The description of an observer illustrates the unsurpassed beauty and the dignity of the ceremonies:

> The ministering of the priests was absolutely unsurpassable in its vigor and the arrangement of its well-ordered silence: All work hard of their own accord, with much exertion, and each one looks after his appointed task. Their service is unremitting, sharing the sacrifices, some undertaking the carrying of wood, others oil, others wheaten flour, others the sweet spices, others offering burnt offerings of the parts of the flesh—all of them exerting their strength in different ways. •They divide the legs of the bullocks with both hands, though they are more than two talents in weight in almost every case, and then with an upward movement rip off with each hand in an amazing way a sufficiently large portion with unerring accuracy. The sheep and the goats are similarly treated in a remarkable way, weight and fat notwithstanding. Those whose concern it is choose in every case spotless specimens outstanding for fatness: Thus the aforesaid procedure is carried out. •They have a rest room set aside, where those who are resting sit down. When this happens, some of those who are rested stand up with alacrity, but no one orders the arrangements of their ministry. •A general silence

reigns, so that one might think that there was not a single man in the place although the number of ministers in attendance is more than seven hundred, in addition to a large number of the assistants bringing forward the animals for sacrifice: Everything is carried out with reverence and in a manner befitting supreme divinity. •It was an occasion of great amazement to us when we saw Eleazar engaged on his ministry, and all the glorious vestments, including the wearing of the "garment" with precious stones upon it in which he is vested; golden bells surround the hem (at his feet) and make a very special sound. Alongside each of them are "tassels" adorned with "flowers," and of marvelous colors. •He was clad in an outstandingly magnificent "girdle," woven in the most beautiful colors. On his breast he wears what is called the "oracle," to which are attached "twelve stones" of different kinds, set in gold, giving the names of the patriarchs in what was the original order, each stone flashing its own natural distinctive color—quite indescribable. •Upon his head he has what is called the "tiara," and upon this the inimitable "mitre," the hallowed diadem having in relief on the front in the middle in holy letters on a golden leaf the name of God, ineffable in glory. The wearer is considered worthy of such vestments at the services. •Their appearance makes one awe-struck and dumbfounded: A man would think he had come out of this world into another one. I emphatically assert that every man who comes near the spectacle of what I have described will experience astonishment and amazement beyond words, his very being transformed by the hallowed arrangement on every single detail.

(Letter to Aristeas 92–99)[2]

Because of the ancient tradition associated with the temple and its ritual, the priests responsible for its administration assumed their role with utmost dedication. Their position at the very focal point of religious devotion afforded them prestige and respect, and occasionally envy, from the common people. In order to maintain the regularity of the temple worship, the priests, and especially the high priest, found it necessary to cooperate with the overlords of their country. By the first century A.D. this had led some to suspect the loyalties of the high priest and his supporters the Sadducees.

These temple leaders heard the voice of the temple. Its beauty and pagentry stimulated their aesthetic and religious sensitivity; their response was dedication. Their life centered in the temple, their energies served the temple, and through it they channelled their devotions to God.

Not only did those engaged in priestly service hear the voice of the temple, but also many common people responded. The daily crowds in the temple, swelling to throngs on holy days, attest to the response of the people. The inestimable budget of the temple was made possible by the annual contributions from far and wide.

The temple had a voice in the life of the people. It spoke through its grandeur, its ceremonies, its religious symbolism, but it surely spoke. Many heard, many responded, and many participated in its life of ritual and ceremony. For them, dedication to the temple indicated their decision for God. But the temple was not the only voice speaking in Palestine.

The synagogue also spoke to the people. When they were in exile after 586 B.C., as the temple lay in ruins, the Jewish people possessed no institution to which to turn for religious devotion. Spontaneously they came together in small groups to discuss their lot. Out of these meetings as the years passed three issues were recognized: (1) The need for a meeting place for instructions and worship; (2) concern to understand the Law; (3) the need for an instructor or expert in the Law. Wherever ten adult Jewish males so desired a synagogue was established. By the first century synagogues dotted Palestine. Some were spacious and elegant, others small and modest; but, whatever the circumstances, its voice was heard by the people.

As an occasion of organized worship, the synagogue's Sabbath services called the people to renew their covenant heritage. The participants in worship recited the *Shema*, or Israel's confession of faith:

> Hear, O Israel: The LORD our God is one LORD; and you shall love the LORD your God with all your heart, and with all your soul, and with all your might. And these words which I command you this day shall be upon your heart; and you shall teach them diligently to your children, and shall talk of them when you sit in your house, and when you walk by the way, and when you lie down, and when you rise. And you shall bind them as a sign upon your hand, and they shall be as frontlets between your eyes. And you shall write them on the doorposts of your house and on your gates.
>
> (Dt. 6:4–9)

Prayers and psalms were a significant part of the liturgy, but foremost in the service was the reading of the Torah, which was accompanied by a selection from the Prophets. During the first century the Torah, that is, the first five books of the OT, was divided into 154 lessons to be read successively until the completion of the Torah. Then the cycle began again. The purpose was to keep ever before the people the Law of God as recorded in their Scriptures.

But simply reading the ancient texts is never enough. The precepts must be clearly articulated and made relevant to the contemporary situation. A significant part of the synagogue service was the discussion of the Torah. This involved the interpretation and application of the selection read on a given Sabbath. If, for example, the section from Deuteronomy was read regarding the putting away of one's wife, how should it be interpreted to the first-century hearer? For those who accept the authority of a document framed in a bygone day it is necessary to reapply it in each new generation lest the importance of the document be lost. It is to the credit of the leaders among the Jews that they developed an institution which provided the place where the Law was interpreted and made relevant to the people.

Of course not every Jew had either the time or the talent to analyze carefully each sentence of the Law and to articulate his own understanding. Thus, very early, some distinguished themselves as gifted in the art of interpretation. Such a person became known as a legal expert or scribe (Gk. *grammateus*), and later rabbi. In the OT Ezra is honored as the first scribe (Neh. 8:1). Scribes of the first century gave themselves to the diligent study of the Law under the tutelage of some older recognized scribe. They heard the interpretation of the great rabbis before them and added their own understanding to the Law. The goal was always to understand the ancient Law and make it applicable to each new generation. It was the scribe or rabbi who usually commented on or explained the Law at a Sabbath service. In the first century, however, any adult male recognized by the synagogue president, might discuss the day's lesson from the Law.

Some of the interpretations of the ancient rabbis were recorded. These provide some insight into how the laws were reapplied from time to time:

> A great general rule have they laid down concerning the Sabbath: whosoever, forgetful of the principle of the Sabbath, committed many acts of work on many Sabbaths, is liable only to one Sin-offering; but, if mindful of the principle of the Sabbath, he yet committed many acts of work on many Sabbaths, he is liable for every Sabbath [which he profaned]. If he knew that it was the Sabbath and he yet committed many acts of work on many Sabbaths, he is liable for every main class of work [which he performed]; if he committed many acts of work of one main class, he is liable only to one Sin-offering.

> The main classes of work are forty save one: sowing, plough-
> ing, reaping, binding sheaves, threshing, winnowing, cleans-
> ing crops, grinding, sifting, kneading, baking, shearing wool,
> washing or beating or dyeing it, spinning, weaving, making
> two loops, weaving two threads, separating two threads, tying
> [a knot], loosening [a knot], sewing two stitches, tearing in
> order to sew two stitches, hunting a gazelle, slaughtering or
> flaying or salting it or curing its skin, scraping it or cutting it
> up, writing two letters, erasing in order to write two letters,
> building, pulling down, putting out a fire, lighting a fire,
> striking with a hammer and taking out aught from one domain
> into another. These are the main classes of work: forty save one.
>   (Mishnah, *Moed, Shabbath*, 7:1, 2 [Danby])[3]

This reveals the effort of the ancient scribes to make the law
regarding Sabbath observance understandable and relevant to
their generation. Many examples of their comments on other
subjects such as marriage, divorce, and the extent of liable could
be given.

The scribes and rabbis formed one chord of the voice of the
synagogue. They helped articulate the message of the synagogue
to the people. Alongside these stood a sect known as the Pharisees,
devout laymen completely dedicated to both the ot Law and to
the implementation of the scribal interpretation. For them the
synagogue worship with its instruction was the focal point of
their religion. It gave form and relevance to the ancient Law. Its
structured services provided a source of encouragement and
strength; furthermore, it provided a podium from which the elite
Judaism could address the partially committed, the apathetic, and
even the Gentile. The synagogue, with its emphasis on worship
and instruction, with its effort to relate the past to the present,
with its challenge to follow God through the keeping of the Law,
was a live option in first-century Palestine. Its voice gave a clear
sound: although the people of Israel had not kept God's Law,
there were those who would instruct in the Law so all Israel could
know the precepts of God. The voice of the synagogue called man
to respond to God through a dedicated effort to understand and
carry out the Law. This was not an effort to create a new and alien
religion; neither was it a novel movement designed to attract
attention. The synagogue was the very finest expression of Judaism
appealing to its own and beyond its own. The voice of the
synagogue summoned listeners to a decision—a decision for the
Law—a decision for God. But this was only one of the voices
heard in Palestine during the early first century.

The discordant voice of the *Qumran Community* sounded apart from the voices of the temple and synagogue, for it had reacted, to some degree, against both. This unique community was comprised of those who, for various reasons, were unwilling to accommodate their religious convictions to the religious, social, and political attitudes of the day. Reactionary groups and isolationists appear occasionally in the history of Israel. For example, the Rechabites in the OT could not adjust to the more sedentary life of the tribes as they emerged into a kingdom under David and Solomon.

When individuals or groups discover that their conclusions, convictions, or religious commitments radically contradict their immediate environment, they must try to change the environment, adjust their convictions, or seek a new environment more compatible with their perspective. This is precisely the action taken by several groups from among the Hebrews. The Qumran community that existed in an out of the way place at the northwest corner of the Dead Sea from the last quarter of the second century B.C. to A.D. 68 best illustrates this response.[4]

In the second century B.C. several events occurred in Palestine that might have prompted a group to withdraw. In 198 B.C. the political control of Palestine fell into the hands of the Seleucids or Syrians of Antioch. This kingly house was not only politically and militarily aggressive but also culturally assertive. They imported new ideas and ways into the land of Palestine. Some Jews were delighted; others were offended, especially at those fellow Jews who fraternized with the new ways. As a result of this cultural aggression there arose a reactionary group known as the "Pious Ones," who sought to hold on to their religious beliefs unchanged. They were completely dedicated to the Law of God and the temple worship where the high priest was chief functionary.

In 171 B.C. the murder of the high priest, Onias III, brought to a close what some considered as the legitimate priesthood, which supposedly had been handed down in the family of Zadok since the days of David. Others not from this family gained the office of high priest. How could one worship God with a fraudulent priesthood? Later when the temple was religiously desecrated by the Syrian troops in 167 B.C. (see 1 Maccabees 1:54), the "Pious Ones" were doubly offended.

When the Jews won their freedom in 164 B.C. through the leadership of the family known as the Maccabeans, the "Pious

Ones" took heart. They felt that God might now restore matters to the true way; however, this did not transpire. Instead, it seemed to them that matters worsened, especially when one of the Jewish rulers usurped to himself the title of high priest. Since he was not of the priestly line of Zadok, this dashed the hopes of those dedicated to the Law, and at the same time it removed the immediate possibility of carrying out true worship from the temple and its ceremonies.

What alternative did those dedicated to the Law have? The office of kings was corrupt. The king was obviously not concerned about the laws of God, and the temple was surely not the proper place of worship, because the priesthood was corrupt. Could God work in this situation? Could a pious person really serve God? The answer for some was a definitive No!

During the reign of the Jewish king, John Hyrcanus I (135–104 B.C.), a group of pious Jews, led by priests from the lineage of Zadok, retreated to an isolated area northwest of the Dead Sea to a place now called Khirbet Qumran. Their own Manual of Discipline explains why they withdrew:

> The Order for all the men of the community who offer themselves to return from all evil and to hold fast to all that he has commanded according to his will.

> They shall separate from the gathering of the men of perversity to join the community in Law and in property; submit to the authority of the sons of Zadok, the priests who keep the covenant, according to the majority of the men of the community who hold fast to the covenant (on their authority shall go forth the decisive edict on every matter of law, property and precept);

> practise truth in community with humility, righteousness and justice, love of mercy and walking humbly in all their ways. No man shall walk in the stubbornness of his heart to stray after his own heart and eyes and the cunning of his own inclination, but he shall in community circumcise the foreskin of his inclination and his stiff neck;

> lay a foundation of truth for Israel to make a community of an eternal covenant;

> make atonement for all who offer themselves to holiness in Aaron or to the house of truth in Israel and those who join them in community;

> in dispute and in judgment to pronounce guilty all who transgress the ordinance.

> this is the course of their ways, according to all these ordinances, when they join the community.

> Everyone who approaches the council of the community shall
> enter the covenant of God in the sight of all who offer
> themselves; and he shall take upon his soul with a binding
> oath to return to the Law of Moses, according to all that he
> commanded, with all his heart and all his soul, and to all that
> has been revealed from it to the sons of Zadok, the priests who
> keep the covenant and who seek out his will, according to the
> majority of the men of their covenant who offer themselves in
> community to his truth and to walk according to his will.
>
> (1QS 5:1–10)[5]

From this paragraph it is obvious that they are withdrawing
from the evil environment of life, from the other Jews who were
not concerned for righteousness. They were assembling a community willing to place the Law foremost in their total existence.
They would not only keep the Law, but would diligently study it
so God's will could speak through the Law.[6]

This community equipped itself with a special room called a
scriptorium where scribes repaired or perhaps copied the precious
scrolls from which they studied the Law. Like the scribes and
Pharisees, they expanded or interpreted the laws of the OT to
apply to their situation. The Zadokite priests were officially in
charge of interpreting the Scriptures to the remainder of the
community. This was in accordance with an OT tradition that
pictures the priest in the role of interpreter[7]

All of this emphasizes that the Law formed the basis of the
community, but the Law was joined to the priesthood. There now
existed in the community a legitimate priesthood as over against
the fraudulent priesthood of the temple cultus. This permitted
the community to transfer the significance of the Jerusalem
temple to its own precincts. The legitimate temple symbolized the
presence of God. Now that they had organized a legitimate
priesthood, who led this reconstituted community, God's presence
could dwell in them; thus they could be looked upon as the "new
temple." The two groups in the community, the laity and the
priesthood, correspond to the Holy Place and the Holy of Holies
in the temple. Since the community no longer recognized the
efficacy of the temple sacrifice the reasonable substitute became a
life lived in complete obedience to every teaching of the Law.[8]

The community, based on the Law with a continued emphasis
on the true meaning of the temple, considered that it constituted
the legitimate covenant people—the true Israel. The Feast of
Pentecost annually recalled the giving of the Law, the covenant,
at Mt. Sinai. This period was especially important to the members
of Qumran, for it was at this season that they renewed their

covenant with God. They were the truly chosen people, the faithful remnant.[9]

Further, this community believed that it was living in the last days and that God's intervention was near. When it came, they would be his instrument to help defeat the evil forces. They would share in the struggle against the evil ones. This would take place at the beginning of the messianic era.[10]

The voice of this group was heard—a voice challenging the normal routine of the temple as well as the synagogue's willingness to be content in an evil generation. It called men to please God by separating themselves from the perverse generation and by actively preparing, through radical devotion to the Law and covenant, for the coming kingdom in whose emergence they would have a part. Whenever people heard the voice of Qumran, they were challenged to decision.

The voice of the *Zealot* also echoed through the hills of Palestine. Perhaps this was the most radical voice that spoke. Exclusive worship of the one true God and an emphasis upon the centrality of the Law led some to be so zealous for the Law that they would kill even a fellow Jew who blasphemed God.[11] The Apostle Paul, prior to his conversion, is described as one zealous for the Law (Gal. 1:13–14; Phil. 3:6). He not only sought to arrest Christians but as in the case of Stephen, he approved their execution; furthermore, with passionate vehemence he attempted to eradicate the Christian church. All of this was carried out because of his dedication to the Law. After his conversion, those zealous for the Law sought to destroy Paul (Acts 21:20–21; 23:12–14). These Zealots directed their hostility toward Paul because from their perspective he, a Jew, had desecrated the Law of God. He deserved death. Even though Paul and his would-be assassins are not specifically called Zealots, their behavior illustrates the mentality of the Zealot party.

The Zealots looked to heroes of the past as examples of zealous conduct for God and his Law. Simeon and Levi avenged the rape of their sister Dinah because of their zeal for the Law (Genesis 34). Phinehas was enraged by the fraternization of Jewish men with Moabite women and took violent action to arrest it (Num. 25:1–8). Elijah's exploits were remembered (1 Kgs. 18:4; 19:10–14). Mattathias, the one responsible for sparking the Jewish revolt for independence in 165 B.C., was also among the heroes of those zealous for the Law of God (1 Macc. 2:27).

Such an extreme group, who was willing to turn its dedication into militant activities, would continually stimulate the nationalism of a conquered people. For its members Rome was thwarting the will of God. Because the Jews were the object of God's promises, Rome would eventually be punished. Because God had met the efforts of Phinehas, Mattathias, and others with success, the Zealots of the first century A.D. would not hesitate, when the occasion arose, to pit their efforts against any enemy of Jewish nationalism. Such a spirit contributed to the provoking of the Jewish-Roman War of A.D. 66–70. The voice of the Zealots invited those listening to a dedication that could become militantly active.

These were the Voices heard in the first-century Palestine which summoned Jews to decision. All claimed to speak on behalf of God; all endeavored to serve God. Whether the temple cult or the Qumran community, both attempted to please God through acknowledging the place and importance of the priesthood. God became real through this channel. Whether the synagogue service, the Qumran society, or the Zealots, all struggled to make the Law real. Through dedication to the Law, God's will could be discovered and acted upon. For each of these groups, God had spoken and was speaking. People must respond, they must decide, they must hear the voice. Yet another voice pierced the air, a voice among voices—"the voice of one crying in the wilderness."

A Voice of Weal and Woe

The voice of the *prophets* of ancient Israel brought both condemnation and hope, invectives yet invitations. Although a voice like Amos' could declare God's wrath:

> "Fallen, no more to rise,
>   is the virgin Israel;
> forsaken on her land,
>   with none to raise her up." (5:2)

it could also hold out an invitation:

> "Seek me and live"; (5:4)
> . . . .
> Seek the LORD and live; (5:6)
> . . . .
> Seek good, and not evil,
>   that you may live;
> and so the LORD, the God of hosts, will
>   be with you, (5:14)

The voice of a prophet frequently spoke of doom and punishment, but at the same time of forgiveness and potential joy.

These were ancient voices even in first-century Palestine, for the voice of prophecy had disappeared since the days of Malachi. But one called John the Baptist appeared in the wilderness of Judea in about the year A.D. 29 as a "voice crying in the wilderness." The earliest Christians identified him as the prophetic forerunner of the Messiah. Mark applied the words of Malachi to him: "Behold, I send my messenger to prepare the way before me" (Mal. 3:1); and along with Matthew and Luke, Mark further pictures John as fulfilling the role of the prophetic voice of Isaiah 40, which commands that preparation be made for the way of the Lord. For the Gospel writer, John the Baptist was a prophet from God—God's messenger.

The judgements of others throughout the Gospel records describe John as a prophet. On two occasions the name of John is brought into close association with Elijah and "the prophets of old." King Herod (Antipas) is perplexed about the identity of Jesus (Mk. 6:14ff. and parallels), having apparently heard the common gossip that Jesus was John risen, Elijah, or one of the prophets. This suggests that the crowds regarded Jesus as being in a class with the prophets along with John the Baptist. A similar incident occurs when Jesus questions his disciples about his identity (Mk. 8:27ff. and parallels). Here again John, Elijah, the prophets, and Jesus all fall under the same prophetic rubric.

Perhaps the most obvious evaluation of John as a prophet comes from the teachings of Jesus. On one occasion Jesus applies the words of Malachi 3:1 to John, and then goes further to declare that John is more than a prophet, among "those born of women" John is the greatest of all (Lk. 7:24-35). Matthew in a similar context records that Jesus identified John with "Elijah who is to come" (Mt. 11:14). On the Mount of Transfiguration the disciples see Elijah and Moses with Jesus; later they ask Jesus about Elijah's coming. Jesus replies "that Elijah has already come." Then Matthew adds that the disciples knew "that he was speaking to them of John the Baptist" (Mt. 17:13). How much clearer could the Gospel tradition be in classifying John the Baptist in the role of a prophet?

Two other incidental matters augment the idea that John was in the prophetic tradition. Mark 1:6 describes his clothing and diet very similar to the description of Elijah in 2 Kgs. 1:8. Further, John, like prophets before him (e.g., Elijah, Elisha, and Isaiah), gathered about him a band of faithful followers (Mt. 11:1-6;

14:12; Mk. 2:18; 6:29; Lk. 11:1; 7:18-20; cf. Acts 19:1ff.). John was truly accepted by many as an authentic prophet.

John the Baptist executed the prophetic function in that his voice sounded forth in a time of crisis. The prophetic voices of the OT punctuated every critical moment of Israel's history. Nathan spoke to the crisis of David's moral lapse, to the issue of building a temple, to the problem of David's successor. Elijah addressed the issue of whether Israel should serve God or Baal. Amos lamented the ebb of Israel's spiritual life. Jeremiah spoke to a series of political crises which culminated in the struggle with Nebuchadnezzar. Such was the role and calling of the prophet, to serve God in a moment of need. So it was with John the Baptist. He came to Israel when many voices clamored for attention, although they were perhaps not always speaking clearly to the people. Each voice endeavored to direct mankind to God; often this took place at the expense of obscuring God. In deciding for God, should one turn to the temple and its ritual, to the synagogue and its interpretation of the Law, to the Qumran withdrawal, or to the Zealot militantism? The garbled message often received by the inhabitants of Palestine led to the desperate need for a clear, distinct, call to decision. John essayed to cut across the intricate legalities and ritualistic mindsets of his day and to offer the people the authentic choice for God.

John set his message in an eschatological framework, that is, he spoke in terms of the imminent inbreaking of God's dynamic power in such a way as to constitute the culmination of the present era. An event was about to take place that would radically change humanity's relation with God.

Such an event harbored the note of *doom*, and John's message carries this theme. Here John again betrays his kinship with the prophets of old. When Nathan entered the moral crisis of David's household, his word brought doom, "The sword shall never depart from your house" (2 Sam. 12:10). Amos spoke foreboding words to the nation of Israel:

> lest he break out like fire in the house of Joseph, and it devour,
> with none to quench it for Bethel. (Amos 5:6)

Isaiah's voice is even more terrifying:

> "When you spread forth your hands,
>   I will hide my eyes from you;
> even though you make many prayers,
>   I will not listen;
> your hands are full of blood." (Isa. 1:15)

John's voice was equally distressing:

> "You brood of vipers!
> . . . .
> the axe is laid to the root of the trees
> . . . .
> he will baptize with . . . fire
> . . . .
> His winnowing fork is in his hand
> . . . .
> the chaff he will burn with unquenchable fire." (Mt. 3:7-12)

Such is John's statement of the prophetic theme of divine judgement.[12]

In addressing his auditors as "vipers," John raised the question of their motive in coming to hear his message. A snake was crafty and clever, but a "viper" was poisonous, intent on injury, and malicious. To address a group thus was to accuse them of having a basic evil nature and disposition. He is saying their entire approach to life and God is evil and wrong. Can they really believe that they know the way of escape—that their present stance before God is correct?

If he indeed accused the Sadducees and Pharisees, as Matthew records it (3:7), then John called into question the larger program of both synagogue and temple. He questioned whether their approach to God was such as to provide an escape or a favorable verdict in the time of judgement. Had the temple ritual degenerated to a mere formality? Was the commitment to the Law drawing a man closer to the Law or God? John does not accept the way of synagogue or temple as ultimately leading man to God.

John's note of doom is further sounded when he refuses to accept prior prerogatives as valid in the day of judgement. "We have Abraham as our father," means nothing. Past privileges have no affect, for already the doom approaches. The destroyer has his instrument of destruction poised; the destruction will be complete; nothing has been spared. "The axe is laid to the root of the trees; . . . cut down and thrown into the fire" (Mt. 3:10).

Into his message of doom John brought the figure of "he who is coming," intentionally introducing a messianic person into the judgement scene. His part in the imminent doom is a role of judge. He is pictured as one threshing the wheat. The symbol of threshing as judgement is amply attested in the OT (Isa. 41:15f.). Here the judge determines those who are prepared and those who are not. Some are gathered as wheat, others destroyed as wheat burned "with unquenchable fire." The foreboding doom is disastrous. There is no escape.

Why would John declare such a message? As the prophets of old, John's sensitive spirit discerned the contradiction between the "isness" and the "oughtness" within the society in which he lived—a society purporting to be God's people. He heard the many voices of the day, all seeking to please God and thus be prepared for any eventuality; but, for John, they had missed the mark. They all, with their varying emphases, had oriented their way around the temple and the Law and had failed to discover the ultimate claim of God upon them. The organized religious efforts had at times left out the common man, and in their formal ways had walled out some sensitive spirits that might be seeking God. John saw the "isness" as the misdirected energies of those who would contain God in their ways and the "oughtness" as the urgent necessity for human beings to place themselves unreservedly under the judgement of God without any effort to ingratiate oneself to him.

On the other hand, like the prophets before, there is a note of *hope* in John's message. Along with Nathan's condemnation came the promise to David that "your house and your kingdom shall be made sure forever before me" (2 Sam. 7:16). Amos did not leave all hopeless:

> . . . establish justice in the gate;
> it may be that the LORD, the God of hosts,
>   will be gracious to the remnant of Joseph. (Amos 5:15)

Isaiah could offer hope to the people he had indicted:

> "Come now, let us reason together,
>   says the LORD:
> though your sins are like scarlet,
>   they shall be as white as snow;
> though they are red like crimson,
>   they shall become like wool." (Isa. 1:18)

Like the prophets before him doom was only one side of John's message, the other side was hope.

John's hope centered in "the mightier one coming after him." He heightens the role of this messianic figure by suggesting that he, John, is not worthy to render the service of a slave to him. John's reference further stresses the imminence of his coming. The eschatological event is already at hand.[13] This messianic figure will baptize with fire and Holy Spirit. There is still somewhat of a threat in the reference to fire, for this is a symbol of judgement both in the context ("thrown into the fire," Mt. 3:10, and "burn with unquenchable fire," Mt. 3:12) and the background of the OT where the prophets and others use "fire" in this manner.[14] John declared that the coming one would baptize with fire. This suggests the symbolic nature of the words. John is declaring that the messianic figure will thrust men into a judgement experience.

Alongside of the judgement experience is the experience of the Holy Spirit. If men are judged, they will also receive the Holy Spirit. They will be baptized in the Holy Spirit. They will undergo the presence of the Spirit as an operative force in their existence. Such a promise was long awaited by the prophets and pious of Israel.

In the OT the Spirit rested on men sporadically as a temporary favor. Yet the old covenant lived in the hope that God would pour out his Spirit on all men at the dawn of the new age. This idea is expressed in several OT passages.

> "And it shall come to pass afterward,
>   that I will pour out my spirit on all flesh;
> Your sons and your daughters shall prophesy,
>   your old men shall dream dreams,
>   and your young men shall see visions." (Joel 2:28)

This prophecy of Joel expresses the hope that the Spirit of prophecy will be poured out on all flesh. The verse is taken from a context in which the Day of the Lord was expected. The pouring out of the Spirit would come before the Day of the Lord and be followed by the restoration of Jerusalem. The giving of the Spirit would begin the messianic age, and this is the way in which the early church interpreted this passage and the event of Pentecost (Acts 2:14-47).

In Ezekiel the gift of the Spirit is associated with a sprinkling of clean water, and the idea of cleansing from sin is present.

> "I will sprinkle clean water upon you, and you shall be clean from all your uncleannesses, and from all your idols I will cleanse you. A new heart I will give you, and a new spirit I will put within you; and I will take out of your flesh the heart of stone and give you a heart of flesh." (Ezk. 36:25f.)

> "And I will put my Spirit within you, and you shall live, and I will place you in your own land; then you shall know that I,

the Lord, have spoken, and I have done it, says the Lord."
(Ezk. 37:14)

It is within the context of the hope of a new age that these expectations are stated.

Second Isaiah has expressed this hope also,

"For I will pour water on the thirsty land,
   and streams on the dry ground;
I will pour my Spirit upon your descendants,
   and my blessing on your offspring." (Isa. 44:3)

In the Isaiah scroll from Qumran a significant passage reads:

Just as many were astonished at thee,
So have I anointed his visage more than any man,
and his form than the sons of men,
So shall he sprinkle many nations because of
himself, and kings shall shut their mouths . . .
(Isa. 52:14f.; 1QIs^a 44:1-4)[15]

This passage may suggest the idea of the Messiah baptizing others with the Spirit.[16] That the Qumran community considered the Spirit to have regenerative effects is evident from the Manual of Discipline:

But God in the secrets of his prudence and glorious wisdom has granted that there shall be a period to the existence of perversity and at the fixed time of its visitation he will destroy it for ever. Then shall come forth for ever truth upon the earth, for it has been contaminated with the ways of evil during the dominion of perversity until the set time which has been decreed for judgment. Then God in his truth will make manifest all the deeds of man and will purify for himself some from mankind, destroying all spirit of perversity, removing all blemishes of his flesh and purifying him with a spirit of holiness from all deeds of evil. He will sprinkle upon him a spirit of truth like waters for purification from all abominations of falsehood and his contamination with the spirit of uncleanness. Thus will upright ones understand knowledge of the highest and impart the wisdom of the sons of heaven to the perfect of way; for God has chosen them for an eternal covenant and for them is all the glory of Adam, all perversity being gone. All deeds of treachery will be put to shame.
(1QS 4:18-23)[17]

The connection between the Messiah and his power to baptize with the Holy Spirit is not clearly delineated; however, in the hope of the age to come there are both the idea of the Messiah, who will deliver, and also the idea of regeneration by the Holy Spirit. John the Baptist is the last of the prophets to express the hope of the outpouring of the Spirit, and he connected it with the Messiah-deliverer.

John's hope of the Messiah who will bring the blessing of the Holy Spirit is a part of the message of doom and judgement. For him there was no other way. To rectify a wrong situation demanded sane judgement, but out of the judging process would come the blessing of the Spirit for those who were alert to the possibility.

To all that John is saying the hearers must make a *decision*. What is their decision regarding this message of doom and hope? The demand is repent: "Repent, for the kingdom of heaven is at hand" (Mt. 3:2). All that John had said about doom and hope, a Messiah executing judgement and bringing the Spirit, meant the kingdom was approaching. The only sensible reaction for men was to accept it—accept the validity of John's message, believing that the kingdom with its Messiah of judgement and hope was at hand.

To make a decision in favor of John's declaration called for a deliberate change of mind and orientation for many who heard. The scribe and Pharisee would have to adjust their thinking about the Law; the priest about the temple; the Qumran people about their way of life; the Zealot about his militant attitude. For, if the kingdom and Messiah are at hand, many religious efforts become obsolete. So also the uncommitted would be challenged to change his mind. Life's new orientation would be the kingdom and its imminence. Only those who deliberately decided in favor of the kingdom would pass through the judgement to benefit from the Spirit.

This deliberate change of mind is what John meant when he said "Repent." The best understanding of this word is *"a call to make a moral decision between two alternative courses set before one."* [18] This does not rule out the idea of turning from sin; for, when one turns to the right relation with God, one must, to some extent, turn from sins for which one feels remorse. Yet the main challenge from John was that the people make a deliberate choice in favor of the kingdom.

A repentance or a decision for the kingdom implied a demonstration of the decision. Those who were willing to accept the imminence of the kingdom, its Messiah of judgement and hope, must so reorient their lives that actions compatible with their decision would be obvious. As the crowds, including tax collectors and soldiers came to him, John amplified the meaning of decision to include proper conduct. They must demonstrate the validity of their decision.

Along with decision and demonstration John demanded that the people undergo his baptism—a baptism of water. Was it too a demonstration of one's decision? This question becomes the subject of the next chapter.

§

There were many voices clamoring for the attention of men in Palestine in the first century A.D., the temple, the synagogue, the Qumran community, the Zealots, and others—all supposing to lead men to God, all laying claim to the way to ultimate truth, all having some outward form of religious ceremonies.

Then there was John's voice—a voice among voices, calling men and women to his claim of the kingdom and its Messiah. It was an urgent message for the time was short, judgement was near, the coming one was already on the threshhold. Men must respond—Repent! John's only formal religious ceremony was baptism. Whence did it come? What did it mean?

1
NOTES

1. Josephus, *Antiquities*, 15.380-425.

2. Translation from "Letter of Aristeas," *The Old Testament Pseudepigrapha* (Garden City: Doubleday and Company, 1985), 2:19.

3. Translation from H. Danby, *The Mishnah* (Oxford: University Press), 102.

4. T. Fritsch, *The Qumran Community* (New York: Macmillan, 1956), 16-25.

5. Translation from A. R. C. Leaney, *The Rule of Qumran and Its Meaning* (London: SCM Press, Ltd., 1966), 161, 169.

6. Ibid., 171.

7. Ibid., 69f.; cf. Dt. 17:8-13, 18; Neh. 8:1-9, 13-15; Ezra 7:10, 11, 13.

8. B. Gartner, *The Temple and the Community in Qumran and the New Testament* (Cambridge: At the University Press, 1965), ch. 2.

9. Leaney, *The Rule of Qumran*, 104-107.

10. K. Schubert, *The Dead Sea Community* (London: Adam & Charles Black, 1959), 91.

11. W. R. Farmer, "Zealots," *IDB*, (1962), 4:936-39.

12. The following interpretation of John's two sayings of judgement is dependent upon C. H. Kraeling, *John the Baptist* (New York: Charles Scribner's Sons, 1951), 33ff.

13. V. Taylor, *The Gospel According to St. Mark* (London: Macmillan, 1959), 156.

14. C. H. H. Scobie, *John the Baptist* (Philadelphia: Fortress, 1964), 67ff., where he quotes Amos 7:4, Mal. 4:1; Ezk. 38:22; et al.

15. Translation from W. H. Brownlee, "John the Baptist in the New Light of Ancient Scrolls," in *The Scrolls and the New Testament*, ed. K. Stendahl (New York: Harper & Brothers, 1957), 43.

16. Ibid., 43f.

17. Translation from Leaney, *The Rule of Qumran*, 154.

18. J. W. Bowman, *The Intention of Jesus* (Philadelphia: Westminster, 1943), 31; cf. 29–33 for interpretation of "repent."

2 | *The Drama of Decision*

Events and decisions that change the course of one's life have a way of becoming dramatized in human society. Most societies dramatize entering adulthood, contracting marriage vows, becoming a parent, assuming public office, etc. Fraternal and religious groups dramatize the candidate's willing decision to enter into full membership through initiation ceremonies. Ceremonies and rituals dramatize and reinforce the decisions and intention of the participant. This nolds true for the ancient rituals of the Hebrew people, including those practices which involved the use of water.

Prologue to the Drama

Water is the source of human existence; with its abundance man prospers, without it man famishes. In a land where rains are not regular, springs go dry and brooks cease to flow, the interest in water becomes acute. It is understandable, therefore, that in the history of Israel perennial springs, ever-running brooks, and wells that did not run dry were considered special gifts from God (Gen. 26:22; Num. 21:16–18; Dt. 6:11; 2 Kgs. 19:24). It was understood by the ancient Hebrew mind that God had controlled the waters of the universe from the very beginning, for in the Genesis account of creation God's Spirit moves over the "face of the waters" (Gen. 1:2), and he separates them that earth may come into existence (Gen. 1:6ff.). So it was proper for Elijah in his contest with the Baalites on Mt. Carmel to demonstrate that his God controlled the "waters above the earth" (1 Kings 18). The fact that the ancient Hebrews recognized the urgency of securing adequate water supplies and that ultimately God controlled all waters may suggest how water became a prominent symbol in the cultic practices of Israel.

The Old Testament affords ample illustrations of the importance of water in religious rites. There were occasions when therapeutic power was mediated through water.[1] When Naaman, the Syrian general afflicted with leprosy, came to Elisha for healing, the prophet sent him to the waters of the Jordan where he dipped himself (Heb. *ṭabal*, LXX *baptizō* 2 Kgs. 5:14) seven times. At first it might appear that the waters of the Jordan possessed some magical power; however, Naaman gives the credit not to the waters but to the God of Israel (2 Kgs. 5:16). The dipping of Naaman expressed his confidence in the God of Israel, and it provided an occasion for the manifestation of God's power. It dramatized his decision to submit to the power of the Hebrew God. Even in NT times the belief existed that the pool of Bethzatha (Bethesda) was occasionally possessed with remedial forces. The story of Jesus' healing of the lame man in John 5 is set in this context.

The place of water in the religious practices of Israel is further illustrated by its use in certain rites of purity. In the thinking of the ancient Hebrews there were things and circumstances that were opposed to an appropriate relation to God. In some mysterious way a person would be rendered unclean, i.e., unfit for participation in the ceremonies relating him to God, if he found himself in certain conditions. If one touched a leper or a corpse, he was unclean. A woman was impure for a prescribed number of days after a menstrual period, an irregular emission, or childbirth; and anyone touching her or her clothing was impure. A man with an irregular discharge was also impure, even during the course of normal sexual relations. These and other conditions placed an individual outside the normal routines of life, both in his relation to his fellowman and in his relation to God.

The Laws of Purity (Leviticus 11–16) are quite explicit in prescribing the conditions by which one was restored to a normal place in society. Sometimes it included isolation for a period, sometimes sacrifice, but always washing in water. In one case it prescribes that "he shall bathe his body in running water" (Lev. 15:13). In some mysterious way water was the occasion whereby the barrier of impurity was removed and the proper relation renewed. The washing in water was not the only part of the prescription for cleanliness, but it was the culminating event.

After other conditions were met, the bathing climaxed the process. Always the individual had to choose to submit to the conditions of restoration.

There were many times when water was used in the cult ceremonies of ancient Israel. A rite of purification with water accompanied an installation to office. The coronation ceremonies for kings probably included a cleansing ritual at the Gihon Spring to prepare the king for receiving the final anointing.[2] Washing with water was prerequisite to Aaron's installation as high priest (Lev. 8:6). The priests were officially dedicated to their vocation with a ritual bath (Num. 8:5-13), and prior to their performing various tasks in their temple it was necessary first to purify themselves through the washing with water (Lev. 16:4, 24, 26). On the Day of Atonement the high priest first bathed himself before proceeding with the ritual which brought him into the presence of God. Upon completion of the ceremony he washed himself again (Lev. 16: 4, 24). The Mishnah (*Yoma* 3. 2-3) records that the high priest underwent five immersions and ten washings on the Day of Atonement.[3] All of this was done that the priest might be acceptable to enter the presence of God. In some mysterious way water removed the profane from the priest and allowed him to enter the precincts of the sacred.

Even when the common man brought a sacrifice to the temple, he must be certain of his state of cleanliness before eating of the sacrifice (Lev. 7:19-21). In fact most of the laws of purity mentioned above came to apply primarily to temple worshippers in the period toward the Christian era.[4] This is not to say that lustrations were not practiced elsewhere, for certain pious Pharisees immersed every morning that they might be pure for daily prayers, the study of the Torah, and meals.[5]

Other occasions of how water functioned in the religious life of Israel can be given, such as the carrying of water from the Pool of Siloam to the altar in the temple at the Feast of Tabernacles as a prayer for rain, a recognition that God is the source of life-giving water. Yet in all the religious practices involving water, the intent seems to be the conditioning of oneself properly to stand in the presence of God. The conditioning of oneself with water was the response of the individual to the challenge of meeting God in the worship ceremonies of ancient Israel. Naaman dipped himself in the Jordan and met God's power. The leper immersed himself in water and was fitted for worship. The high priest bathed himself and entered the sanctuary of God. Yet it is not to be supposed that the only concern was for the outward drama of the cleansing rituals. Prophets like Isaiah could speak of washings and inner purity (Isa. 1:16f.). Zechariah (13:1) and Ezekiel (36:25f.) speak of the time that God will cleanse in his own way when he will sprinkle with clean water. Jewish writings of the first century A.D. confirm that the cleansing rituals had a connection with moral purity.[6] The Hebrews of this period, following the ancient customs of the Law and temple, continued to give expression to their efforts to remain in proper fellowship with God through the practice of water rituals.

The previously mentioned *Qumran community* of the Essenes, as protestors against the Jerusalem temple and its priesthood, continued many of the practices of Jewish ritual, including ritual bathing. Josephus' description of Essenes makes it quite clear that initiated members bathed daily as a means of purification.[7] That branch of the Essenes known as the Covenanters of Damascus gives specific instructions in its manual regarding purification by water. Emphasis is placed on the amount of water necessary for purification.[8] In the Qumran Manual of Discipline several references are made to ritual ablutions.[9] From their writings it appears that a novice, after preliminary examination, served for one year. Upon a second examination he was admitted to his first ritual bath. This, of course, would have unique significance since it introduced him to more privileges within the group, including participation in subsequent water lustrations. After a second year's probation and a satisfactory review by the group, the candidate was accepted into full membership.

As important as these ritual baths were, the Essenes always emphasized the precondition of the participant. Those refusing the covenant could find no hope in formality:

> He will not be made guiltless by atonement and he will not be purified in waters of purification; he shall not sanctify himself in seas or rivers nor will he be purified in all the waters of cleansing. Unclean, unclean shall he be all the days of his rejection of the precepts of God with its refusal to discipline himself in the community of his counsel.
>
> (1QS 3:3–6)

> (Such a man) shall not enter the waters to approach the purity of the men of holiness, for men will not be purified except they turn from their wickedness, for uncleanness clings to all transgressors of his word.
>
> (1QS 5:13f.)[10]

In their effort to establish the true people of God the Essenes sought to carry forward their dedication to the Law and temple as mentioned above. Along with this they continued the customs of water ablutions as practiced in the temple according to the Law. Yet they did not depend upon the act itself. The water baths were to be accompanied by the proper disposition. The initial lustration verified the authenticity of the novice's commitment. It dramatized his decision to subject himself to the ways of the group. It gave evidence of his purity.

The use of water in religious rituals not only applied to true Hebrews but also to those Gentiles who became a part of the Jewish community. The first ritual required of a proselyte was circumcision. It would naturally follow that they would choose to be pure in order to participate in all the privileges of their new religion. Perhaps out of this very natural submission to the regular Jewish lustrations there grew up the custom of *Jewish proselyte baptism* which had a different significance than the recurring baths of purification.

The discussions in Jewish literature of the initiatory ritual for Gentiles describe three steps: circumcision, baptism, and the making of an offering at the temple. Circumcision did not apply to women, and after A.D. 70 offerings at the temple were impossible, thus baptism received additional attention. An adequate description of the baptismal practice can be given. Running water was preferred but, if not available, other provisions could be made so long as the amount was sufficient, approximately 120 gallons. The candidate was to participate in the nude to assure complete contact with the water. In the case of women their hair should not be braided but left loose. The individual immersed himself; no one was touching the initiate as he went under the waters. At least two male witnesses were present. They reminded the proselyte of the seriousness of the step he was taking and, while he stood partly immersed, they recited portions of the Law to him. In the case of women initiates care was taken to preserve modesty. The male witnesses stood behind a curtain or screen while a female attendant directed the ceremony. All of this was done during the daylight hours.[11]

What did such a ceremony mean to those who chose to submit to it? It was their initiation into the Jewish faith. It was the drama of their decision. It was their affirmation of the validity of the Jewish way of life that took its form and destiny from God. The rite expressed complete dedication to God. The fact that the male witnesses reminded the candidate of the seriousness of the situation suggests that the spiritual condition of the initiate was important. The person being baptized must have pure motives for the rite alone could not change his disposition. This is not to minimize the act of baptism. The rabbis looked upon the proselyte as a new-born child entering upon a new life and regarded baptism as the rite dramatizing that new beginning.

It is not until the end of the first century A.D. that such a description of proselyte baptism as derived from Jewish literature becomes clear. The exact stage of development of the practice a century earlier can only be inferred. Since the rabbinic schools of Hillel and Shammai debated the matter, it may be that the founders of the schools did also, thus suggesting the presence of the practice early in the first century.[12] It is far less likely that the Jews would have developed a rite patterned after the Christians than the reverse. Thus, because the Hebrews employed water as a significant symbol in their religious practices, they also utilized this symbol in their rite for admitting Gentiles. There it served as a tangible expression of the decision to adopt the Jewish faith. It dramatized the birth of a new Israelite.

The Center Stage Drama

John the Baptist stood in the center of the religious stage in first-century Palestine proclaiming a message of doom and hope, of repentance and conduct corresponding to repentance, a message calling for a decision demonstrated in the rite of baptism. Like the pious Hebrew, the temple priest and worshipper, and the Essenes of Qumran, John used water in a religious rite. Had he simply borrowed from them, or did he originate a completely new practice?

The mechanics of John's baptism are obvious. Those who came to him and so chose were baptized by him, i.e., they were plunged under the water, immersed in the waters of the Jordan. This is what "baptize" means. The word was used in ancient literature to mean "dip" or "plunge," with the idea of being completely overcome or overwhelmed.[13] There is no doubt that those who presented themselves to John were plunged under the water of the Jordan. But what did it mean? This is as important as the process of the rite.

From simply being an informed Hebrew *John the Baptist would be aware of the Laws of Purity* (Leviticus 11–16) and the practice in the temple and by righteous Hebrews; but, in addition to this, John came from a priestly family (Lk. 1:5), making his acquaintance with the laws of purity and water baths more definite. He was well aware of the water rituals meticulously observed by the priests in Jerusalem who hoped to fit themselves for service before God in the temple. He knew how the pilgrims entering Jerusalem cleansed themselves in anticipation of their standing before God in his holy sanctuary.

Now John declared that the people must stand ready to confront God in judgement by the One about to appear. The final eschatological event approached. The kingdom is near, men will meet God. As the participant in the temple worship prepared to meet God through water ablutions, John prepared his followers to meet God through his water rite. Those who practiced water rituals in their homes or at the temple were well aware of the necessity of sincere motives and attitudes prerequisites to the act. John, like the prophets before him, insisted upon sincerity and conduct demonstrative of genuine commitment to his challenge.

While John's requirements resembled the regular ablutions, there were some striking differences. John does not stress the exact point of uncleanness. He has no apparent concern for the previous experiences or attitudes of the participant with purificatory washing. Anyone and everyone could respond to John's challenge. Pharisees and Sadducees—no matter how ritually pure according to their interpretations—priests from Jerusalem, tax collectors scorned by their fellow Hebrews, and soldiers with little knowledge of purity and impurity, all came to the baptism on an equal footing as far as John was concerned. All of this transpired in a public place—not in the privacy of an individual's home or in the temple precincts. Yet this alone does not confirm a vast difference in the use of the water rite by John and the traditional practice, for both prepared for or pointed to further participation. The significant difference is that to which each pointed. The traditional practice prepared the individual to approach God through morning prayers, Torah study, or temple worship, while John's baptism pointed to the inbreaking of the kingdom, the arrival of its Messiah, and his accompanying judgement. John's baptism was an integral part of his larger challenge of the traditional interpretation of the temple and synagogue of the religion of Israel.

Since there are some interesting *parallels between John the Baptist and the Qumran community,* could it be that they had similar rites of baptism? As already pointed out both John's message and the life of the Qumran disciples challenged the temple and synagogue worship. Both seem quite convinced that they are preparing for a new day in the religious life of Israel. John is pictured in the Gospel as the one preparing the way:

> "the voice of one crying in the wilderness:
> Prepare the way of the Lord,
> make his path straight" (Mk. 1:3)

In the Gospel of John these words come from the lips of the Baptist himself and may very well represent his own interpretation of his mission. This quotation is from Isaiah 40:3, which is the point of similarity with the Qumran community that sees its role in a similar light:

> And when these exist in a community in Israel, according to this programme they shall be separated from among the settlement of the men of iniquity to go into the desert, to prepare there the way of Him, as it is written,
>   In the wilderness prepare the way of . . . in the Arabah they shall make straight a highway for our God (Isa. 40:3).
>   (1QS 8:12–14)[14]

For this group the place of preparation was the desert and the way of preparation was the proper interpretation of the Law and obedience to it.[15] The Manual makes this quite clear by explaining the quotation of Isaiah 40:3: "This means study of the Law [which] he commanded by the hand of Moses" (1QS 8:15). They understood themselves to be an instrument in the final revelation of God. So also John the Baptist understood himself to have a significant role in the coming of the kingdom; both use Isa. 40:3 to express their roles. When applied to John, *The Voice* in the wilderness is emphasized; when applied to the community, *the way* is emphasized. For both this preparation meant that the inbreaking of God was near.

While there were some similarities, John's baptism was quite different.[16] He neither required a probation period nor a review of the candidate by a group. There is no indication that John required those baptized to be immersed repeatedly. John's respondents were neither rejecting the normal relations of human existence nor seeking a monastic life. Really, the only similarity between John's rite and the Qumran group was the fact that they both immersed. Other than this there is simply nothing about John's baptism that directly relates it to Qumran.[17] The situation is best understood that both have taken their rites from the larger background of the Purity Laws and their practice in Judaism.[18] The significant difference is in the larger context of the teaching of each. For the Qumran Essenes, their initial water bath meant that the individual had proven his sincere intention through the year's probation and was judged by the community worthy of further participation. For John, baptism demonstrated the individual's willingness to submit to the judgement of God.

Now almost simultaneous with the appearance of John, the main line of Judaism was developing *proselyte baptism*. The data are too tenuous to affirm a direct borrowing of one from the other; however, there are certain similarities. Both John and the proselyte ritual demanded complete immersion of the body. Proselyte baptism preferred running water, and John baptized in the Jordan. Even second-century Christians preferred running water. That proselyte baptism may have influenced Christian baptismal practices at a later date is noted by some Christians of the fourth century who require the candidate to be baptized in the nude.[19] In addition to the procedural similarities, the meaning of each had common elements. Jewish proselyte baptism negated all the candidates' previous relationships and loyalties and ushered him into a new life in the household of Israel. John's baptism required a repentance—a turning from one stance to another. Each indicated that a change had taken place in the life of the candidate and that entrance into a new phase in the spiritual pilgrimage had begun. Both baptisms required a proper attitude or disposition toward the meaning of the event. Both insisted on the sincerity of the candidate.

In spite of these similarities there are obvious differences. John did not require circumcision as a prerequisite. Jew and Gentile alike came to his baptism. Nor was John's baptism an effort to fulfill the Laws of Purity. John's baptism was public, requiring neither seclusion nor specified witnesses; lacking formalities, it was simply administered as people came. Unlike the proselyte baptism, John's did not usher his candidates into further ritual activities privileged only to those of a community or a nation. His baptism was not the door into an organized group, only into a movement which he was espousing. Proselyte baptism admitted the initiated into a highly organized Jewish religious life, John had no organization.[20] While the questions of whether John was directly borrowing from Jewish proselyte baptism must remain open, it is obvious that both have developed along somewhat similar lines—with differences—from the same milieu of ritual ablutions.

Moreover, it is quite obvious that John took advantage of the theatrical props of his day to dramatize his message. Water ablutions were much in use in Palestine when he appeared on the scene. The rite already signified that the participant was seeking to establish the right relationship to God. The rite occurred in a religious context and connoted commitment. But how has John used it? His emphasis does not seem to be in creating Levitical purity, preparing one for temple worship, bringing foreigners into Judaism, or establishing a restricted community.

As was noted in chapter one, John was first and foremost a prophet. He declared the condemnation of his generation, but he also offered hope. He boldly proclaimed God's imminent entrance into the affairs of his people, with judgement but with justice, too, at the hands of the "Mightier One." In effect, John announced the messianic kingdom. He challenged his auditors to a positive response—a decision of repentance, a preparation for the crisis. Now this decision must be vividly portrayed. The individual's willing and deliberate response to John's call of repentance must be dramatized.

As the prophets before him John utilized *dramatic acts to vivify his message*. Isaiah on one occasion wrote his message on a scroll and committed it to the keeping of his disciples as a protest against those who had ignored his message (Isa. 8:16); or the ancient prophet could go half clad through the streets of Jerusalem as a portent against Egypt and Ethiopia (Isa. 20:1-6). The conduct of Jeremiah was equally dramatic. Whether he broke a pitcher to dramatize God's breaking of the people and the city (Jer. 19:10) or bought a parcel of ground in the territory occupied by the enemy to prove his hope of restoration (Jer. 32:9), Jeremiah dramatized his message. Ezekiel was especially noted for his dramatic activities. He could picture the seige of Jerusalem on a brick, the punishment of Israel and Judah by lying on his side, the shortage of food by his diet (Ezekiel 4). Such symbolic dramatic actions frequently recur in ot prophetic literature. The acts were performed by the prophet to call attention to his accompanying message. A prophet announcing his message orally would not hesitate to embody that message in concrete action, thus expressing an actuality and reality beyond the spoken word. The dramatic act gave a dimension in time and space to the prophet's declaration.[21]

To dramatize his message John chose the medium of baptism. The message of imminent judgement, an urging of repentance, John dramatized by plunging the respondent under the water of the Jordan. Unlike most of the prophetic actors before him John did not stage the drama alone. The scene could be enacted only as others participated. This focuses attention on the individual involved in the act. The candidate came front and center of the stage to act out his role. He willingly declared himself not just a spectator but a participant in the drama, for indeed the baptism dramatized his decision. The phrase "baptism of repentance" (Mk. 1:4) gives the clue to the participant's involvement. The kind of baptism John offered was characterized by repentance. When it is understood that repentance is a deliberate moral choice between alternate possible courses, then John's baptism can be recognized as the embodiment of that choice.

Baptism is the concrete expression of the moral choice that has been made. It vividly portrays in time and space the inner decision made by the participant. John has carefully chosen a rite demanding participation. Whatever his message, whatever his challenge, its aim was to evoke a positive response from his audience. Whatever dramatization he effected, whatever medium he chose to give vivid presentation to his demand, it was only a prelude to the climax—the willing response of the auditors. For one participating, it was really his drama of decision!

If in the baptism of repentance the individual chose a specific alternative, what was it? In repenting in favor of John's message the candidate rejected as final the religious security offered by the temple and its ceremony, the assurance of acceptability before God through the synagogue and its oral law, the militant course of the Zealots, and the monastic way of Qumran. The ones being baptized even rejected their privileged status as Israelites. They were accepting as valid John's demand to stand under the judgement of God's immediate inbreaking. Whether it brought doom or hope, they were choosing to confront God in the person of the "Mightier than I." They elected to be judged by *him* on *his* terms, claiming no special privilege. This willingness to unconditional confrontation with the messianic figure responded to the core demand of John's message. The decision to submit to this was dramatized in the rite of baptism. The coupling of the imminent appearance of the Messiah with water baptism uniquely occurred in John's message and drama.[22] Although the Qumran people expected the messianic era to appear, it was not as close at hand as John declared.

Why did John choose the rite of baptism to dramatize his message and the decision of the individual? Is there any analogy between the decision and the rite? It is not always possible nor desirous to discover a rational parallel between the meaning experienced and the symbol of that experience. It is interesting that a substance so mysterious as water was used by John. Water could give life, but it could destroy. It was controlled by God, but it was the substance of the fearful regions of the underworld. In some OT texts the writers give evidence of being influenced by Babylonian cosmology which causes them to hint that at creation God manifested his power over the antagonist forces of the universe by forcing them to retreat to the waters of the underworld, which for the Hebrew writers was the place of death (Job 38:16f.; Ps. 74:13f.; 89:10). The prospects of death were never pleasant to them. Yet when they meditated upon their defeat and deliverance by God, the idea of being spared from the waters is present (Ps. 18:16; 42:7; 69:1ff.).[23] Thus to plunge oneself into the depth of the waters representing the unknown fearful arena of death and the underworld where only God is able to defend and deliver could symbolize the individual's decision of unreserved confidence in God whatever the risk. While such an interpretation of baptism relates the decision to the symbol, it is impossible to know that either John or his candidates had this in mind. It remains to accept that John simply used a ritual already at hand to dramatize his message and the response of the individual.

§

John then did not try to organize a new group, a different sect; he was not a militant rebel. He was a prophet with an urgent message: Be willing to meet God's Messiah unconditionally. He sought to dramatize his message as vividly as possible. Using a well-known ritual he plunged individuals under the waters of the River Jordan. But this was an act that required the cooperation and participation of the respondent. Thus the individual was called upon to share in the drama. From the individual's point of view, he heard John's challenge to unconditional confrontation, he repented to John's call, he decided in favor of the authenticity of the message, he was willing to submit to the imminent appearance of the Messiah, he chose to give concrete expression to his response through John's baptism. This was his drama of decision.

2

NOTES

1. J. Thomas, *Le Mouvement Baptiste en Palestine et Syrie* (Gembloux: Universitas Catholica Lovaniensis, 1935), 342–350, suggests the three categories for the discussion of water rites in the ОТ: therapeutic, purity, cult ceremonies.

2. S. Mowinckel, *He that Cometh*, transl. G. W. Anderson (Nashville: Abingdon Press, n.d.), 63; cf. R. de Vaux, *Ancient Israel*, transl. J. McHigh (New York: McGraw-Hill, 1961), 102, for an opposing view that the spring was of primary importance in the coronation ceremony.

3. N. A. Dahl, "The Origin of Baptism," *Interpretationes ad Vetus Testamentum Pertinentes Sigmundo Mowinckel* (Oslo: Fabritius & Sønner, 1955), 36–52, esp. 38.

4. Ibid., 39.

5. Ibid., 41f.

6. Ibid., 40f.

7. *Wars*, 2.128–129.

8. CD 10:10–13.

9. 1QS 3:4–12; 5:7–20; 6:13–23.

10. Transl. from Leaney, *The Rule of Qumran*, 137, 170.

11. For a fuller description and text reference cf. H. H. Rowley, "Jewish Proselyte Baptism and the Baptism of John," *Hebrew Union College Annual* 15 (1940): 320–26; G. F. Moore, *Judaism* 3 vols. (Cambridge: Harvard University Press, 1950), 1:331–35.

12. For this point of view of the date of origin of proselyte baptism, cf. Rowley, "Jewish Proselyte Baptism," 320 and T. F. Torrance, "Proselyte Baptism," *NTS* 1 (1954/5): 154.

13. For lexical studies s.v. βάπτω and βαπτίζω, *BAG* and A. Oepke, "βάπτω, βαπτίζω, κτλ," *TDNT* (1964), 1:529–45. For further interpretation cf. F. Stagg, *New Testament Theology* (Nashville: Broadman, 1962), 205f.; W. F. Flemington, *The New Testament Doctrine of Baptism* (London: S.P.C.K., 1948), 11f.

14. Transl. Leaney, *The Rule of Qumran*, 209.

15. Ibid., 222.

16. For the differences cf. H. H. Rowley, "The Baptism of John and the Qumran Sect," *New Testament Essays*, ed. A. J. B. Higgins (Manchester: University Press, 1959), 222f.

17. Ibid., 223.

18. Ibid., and Dahl, "Origin of Baptism," 44.

19. Rowley, "Proselyte Baptism," 325f. and fn. to church fathers.

20. The Gospel records picture John as one giving way to Jesus; he is only a voice, he intends no ongoing organization. Some of his disciples carried on after his imprisonment and death as evidenced by Mark 6:29 and Acts 19:1–7. When compared with the institutional life of the synagogue, John's activity was spontaneous. From the Gospel records there is no evidence that John is inducting members into an organization.

21. For the interpretation of John's baptism as a prophetic symbol, cf. C. K. Barrett, *The Holy Spirit and the Gospel Tradition* (London: S.P.C.K., 1947), 32f.; Flemington, *Doctrine of Baptism*, 20; A. Gilmore,

"Jewish Antecedents," *Christian Baptism*, ed. A. Gilmore (Philadelphia: Judson, 1959), 75-82; F. J. Leenhardt, *Le Baptême Chrétien son Origine, sa Signification* (Neuchatel: Delachaux & Niestle S.A., 1946), 12f.; Taylor, *Gospel*, 155.

22. Thomas, *Le Mouvement Baptiste*, 86; cf. F. J. Leenhardt, "Jean-Baptiste: sa Predication, son baptême," *Le Cahiers Biblique le foi et Vie* 1 (1936): 37.

23. For an extended discussion of this idea cf. Per Lundberg, *La Typologie Baptismale dans L'Ancienne Église* (Uppsala: A.-B. Lundequistska Bokhandeln, 1942), chapter 2.

3 | *The Willing Response*

What provokes a person to action? What preconditioning culminates in a moment of decision? What sensitivities of the inner being are touched in such a way as to call forth a specific act demonstrating a willing response to a challenge of decision? Such questions may very well be asked of Jesus' willingness to be baptized by John in the Jordan River. The Gospel records are almost completely silent about Jesus' activities prior to his baptism, yet they are most adamant that Jesus was baptized, and that in the context of that experience an understanding of his relation to God became articulate.

From a Searching Heart

Between the birth of Jesus and his appearance before John, the Gospels provide two bits of interesting information. There is the statement by Luke that the family of Jesus resided in Nazareth and "the child grew and became strong, filled with wisdom; and the favor of God was upon him" (Lk. 2:39f.). This is Luke's way of emphasizing that even in *childhood Jesus displayed unusual characteristics.* He had opportunity to do this through participation in the synagogue school at Nazareth where the male children were taught the Law and its meaning for their lives. Under the tutelage of a devout scribe the young boys were made aware of the importantce of their religious heritage; and, through the exemplary life of sincere Pharisees who were most often enthusiastic for the interpretation of the Law which the synagogue fostered, they could witness the living results of that heritage. Coupled with the instructions of pious parents, the synagogue school became the transmitter of Hebrew culture. In such an atmosphere a profound interest in God, his relation to man, and one's own religious destiny might be aroused. Here Jesus "increased in wisdom." Here the sensitive person could search for meaning.

From his earliest years Jesus was aware of the impact that the synagogue, its educational activities and its Sabbath ceremonies, had upon the people. He could have some estimation of its effectiveness among the masses, its need for adjustment and reform, as well as its genuine importance as a conveyor of the past religious experiences of his people with God—the tradition of Abraham, Moses, and the prophets. This institution not only provided the people of the first century with a religious option,[1] it also was a context within which a searching heart could discover direction.

The second bit of information the Gospels record about Jesus prior to his baptism is *his presence in the temple in Jerusalem.* The scene as recorded only by Luke (2:41-51) took place when Jesus was twelve years old, while on a pilgrimage to Jerusalem with his parents to attend the Passover festivities. At age twelve a Jewish boy attained the identity of a Son of the Law.[2] This represented an important juncture in the religious life of the individual; for, henceforth, he was responsible for carrying out the obligations of the Law. So in the temple the young boy, Jesus, found the most reputable of the teachers and questioned them further about the matters with which he had become familiar in his previous religious training. They were amazed not because he was displaying his own omnipotence at the expense of their ignorance but because he was expressing interest and insight by questioning far beyond his age.[3] Such activity displays the spiritual probing on the part of Jesus to discover fully God's intention as it had been set forth in the Hebrew heritage. Jesus' comment to his parents that he must be in his Father's house further emphasizes his determined effort to understand his religious heritage and to fathom the awesomeness of the things of God. By presenting this brief story Luke intended to give the reader an insight into the pre-baptismal experiences of Jesus and in so doing has provided a glimpse of Jesus' searching heart.

Jesus' visit to Jerusalem suggests that he early became aware of the importance of the temple as the center of the religious life of the Hebrews with its emphasis on the well-ordered sacrifices and ceremonies. Any Hebrew reflecting upon the history of the temple would be impressed by the priestly group who so patiently observed the rituals attached to it, for even the Law was explicit in its demands of loyalty to the temple. To the person seeking to relate to God, to one determined to discover God's will, the temple did offer a possibility.[4] Jesus could not have overlooked this.

Neither could Jesus have been ignorant of the miniority movements in Palestine—the Qumran community and the Zealots. These two groups certainly attracted attention to themselves by their radical and, in the case of the Zealots, militant ways.[5] While these sects were not as popular as the synagogue and temple, they were still a religious option that must be considered by the searching heart.

Prior to Jesus' baptism by John, he was confronted with both the popular and less popular way of Judaism's efforts to articulate a meaningful way for man to relate to God. These were a part of Jesus' religious environment. They were the institutions which nurtured his thought in his childhood and early manhood. They provided the experiences and ideas out of which Jesus formulated his own thinking. The first-century religious milieu contributed to the form and content of Jesus' religious decisions expressed in his conduct and teachings. Yet when Jesus chose to declare himself publicly, he chose neither an intimate relation with the synagogue nor the temple, but rather submission to the baptism which John preached. Why?

To an Urgent Demand

From a searching heart Jesus responds to an urgent demand— John's proclamation and baptism. It must be recalled that John took his stand with none of the other voices of his day but rather cast himself in the role of the prophets of old with his message of weal and woe.[6] Furthermore, John's prophetic message was set in an eschatological framework; for him the judgement with its messianic figure was imminent. The only possible escape from the doom of judgement was repentance coupled with baptism and conduct fitting repentance. All of this meant that the kingdom of God was near at hand. That is to say God's eternal presence, his rule over man's will, was a present reality to those who would accept John's declaration. The new era beginning with God's judgement and the presence of his Spirit was no longer a future event; it was already breaking in upon John's generation; and those with a sensitive spirit could prepare for it and undergo its judgements with the preparation of repentance—the deliberate choice to accept John's message as valid. This decision was dramatized in the act of baptism.

Now Jesus deliberately chose to associate with the proclamation of John. For him this was the voice, the religious option, that best actualized his religious thinking. Had Jesus been gleaning from the prophets and become convinced that God's rule, his presence in the lives of people, was governed neither by the temple nor by the Law but by his very presence? Did Jesus feel that over-institutionalization of religion had insulated men from God? Did he hear in the voice of John the calling forth of those who were willing to stand before God's judgement with no claim except that they were willing to accept it? From the previous discussion of his message, it is apparent that John demanded a decision in favor of his proclamation of the imminent judgement of God. He insisted that each person must stand before God alone with no claim other than the willingness to submit to God's judgement. The only legitimate response was repentance and baptism. Certainly Jesus understood John's message, willingly accepted it, and was baptized.

A Decisive Commitment

The question of his own inner purity or sinfulness was not the issue in Jesus' coming to John for baptism. The Gospels do not picture Jesus' coming to John filled with irrational sorrow for sins committed, nor do they picture him declaring his sinfulness. What they do portray is Jesus' decision to be baptized by John. When it is recalled that repentance can best be interpreted as *"a call to make a moral decision between two alternative courses set before one,"* the question of Jesus' sinlessness or emotional sorrow are somewhat beside the point; for his coming to John was Jesus' declaration that John's proclamation was valid. Of all the religious options available at the time, this was the correct one. *Jesus' decision to submit to John's baptism was the proper end of his searching heart* in that he discovered a means to demonstrate his relationship to God. Jesus responded to the urgent demand that man must stand before God without any claim of success at keeping rules or rituals. He responded to the claim that the kingdom of God—the very presence of God—is a reality breaking in upon men. Jesus willingly accepted John's proclamation as authentic.

Why then did John hesistate to baptize Jesus? The Gospel of Matthew records the brief exchange between the two (3:14f.). John humbly suggests that Jesus should baptize him, and Jesus responds that he is seeking to "fulfill all righteousness." Were the two acquainted prior to this event? Had they shared their spiritual searchings and experiences? Did John simply recognize Jesus as a superior soul? Or is John here confessing that Jesus is the "Mightier than I"? Unless this brief dialogue has been inserted by the Gospel writer to soften the idea that Jesus was baptized for his sins,[7] it stands to reason that John did at least recognize Jesus as one of superior spiritual capacities. What is more important is Jesus' statement concerning his reason for coming to John—"to fulfill all righteousness." The clue to the meaning of the word righteousness comes from the beatitude: "Seek first his kingdom and his righteousness." There the exhortation is to submit to the total demand of God and his kingdom—radical obedience to God's will. So when Jesus insists that he must be baptized "to fulfill all righteousness," he is saying that it is the will of God.[8] For him the challenge of John's message was God's voice to his searching heart. In answering that challenge he made the decision of radical obedience to the will of God. Could he stop short of vividly dramatizing his decision through the manner that John had chosen to embody his message. So Jesus, like those before and after him, came to John's baptism to declare publicly his acceptance of God's claim upon himself in the voice of the prophet.

Now the Gospels depict the baptismal event in the life of Jesus as the beginning of his public ministry. In so doing they have not only noted Jesus' relation to John's preaching but have also stressed *the baptism of Jesus as an experience of self-understanding*. The decision to obedience to God through John's proclamation was not only Jesus' commitment, it also became the occasion for understanding his destiny in God's plan. The events immediately following Jesus' baptism—the heavens opening, the voice speaking, the Spirit descending—were the culmination of Jesus' inner search for the will of God for his life.

Following the actual baptismal act, Luke reports that Jesus was praying when the voice of God sounded from heaven. This further emphasizes Jesus' willingness to search diligently for God's will. Each of the first three Gospels describes the heavens opening, the dove descending, the voice speaking. The opening of the heavens is a characteristic feature of apocalyptic literature where, in some visionary way, a revelation is set forth. The heavens represent an impenatrable barrier between God and man, and now that barrier is being split asunder in anticipation of a communication or revelation from God.[9]

The barrier between heaven and earth having been broken, the Spirit (of God) descends on Jesus. The descent is so real that it is described as the flight of a dove. In rabbinic literature the dove is associated with the "daughter of the voice" (*bath qol*) which is an inferior revelation coming to pious individuals after the superior inspiration of the Holy Spirit to the prophets had ceased to be operative.[10] Such an explanation is hardly suitable here, however, for the parting of the heavens emphasizes the uniqueness of the revelation, and the Spirit actually comes to rest upon Jesus. This is no second-class inspiration. To describe the Spirit's descent like a dove (Luke adding "in bodily form," 3:22) is simply a vivid way of stating that the Spirit from God came upon Jesus following his baptism.[11]

It has already been pointed out that endowment with the Holy Spirit was part of the messianic equipment.[12] Furthermore, the Spirit equipped the Servant of Second Isaiah to perform his task for God. In Isaiah 42:1 it is the task of the Servant to bring justice to the nations. To accomplish this mission the Servant is endowed with God's Spirit: "I have put my Spirit upon him." When the Servant poems of Second Isaiah are read together, the several tasks of the Servant are clear: he is the chosen one of God to establish right religion among all nations.[13] The Spirit upon him is a part of the preparation and equipment whereby he will accomplish his mission. Even outside the Servant poems the endowment of the Spirit is upon God's chosen. This is quite obvious in Isa. 61:1-2a:

> The Spirit of the Lord GOD is upon me,
> because the LORD has anointed me
> To bring good tidings to the afflicted;
> he has sent me to bind up the brokenhearted,
> To proclaim liberty to the captives,
> and the opening of the prison to those who are bound;
> To proclaim the year of the LORD's favor.

The opening lines might be paraphrased: "Because God has given me a mission he has endowed me with his Spirit. The mission is to declare the good news of God's concern." Here the anointing, i.e., the appointment to a task, and the gift of the

Spirit go together. A similar description is found in Isaiah 11 where the prophet searches for the ideal leader of Israel—one whose task is to usher in the idyllic age. This one is able to accomplish his task because he is equipped with "the Spirit of the Lord."

The voice from heaven begins by saying: "Thou art my beloved son" (Lk. 3:22). This declaration reflects Psalm 2:7. In this psalm the king of Israel speaks on the occasion of his coronation and relates the oracle or revelation that has come to him. The opening statement of that revelation is: "You are my son." The king is thus brought into the closest possible relation to God as he is installed as God's representative in serving as the temporal head of God's people. That the father-son image is an appropriate description of this relationship is attested by 2 Sam. 7:14 where God speaks through Nathan to David describing his relation to Solomon as that of father to a son. This is the experience of Jesus at his baptism. The revelation that comes to him is that he enjoys the closest possible relation to God. He is God's appointed representative to Israel to complete the assigned task. It cannot be overlooked that the descent of the Spirit echoes the appointment of the Servant to his task in Second Isaiah, while the content of the revelation recalls the coronation of a Davidic king. Yet even the second half of the declaration mirrors the Servant's call of Isa. 42:1, where God describes his chosen as one "in whom my soul delights," a phrase connoting the same abiding affection as "my beloved, in thee I am well pleased."

What has happened in this revelatory experience of the heaven's opening, the Spirit's descending, and the voice's speaking is that Jesus' relation to God has become articulate along with a sense of mission. He now understands his role as that of the Servant who will bring God's good news of righteousness and deliverance to the people. This is especially dramatized in the descent of the Spirit; it is further underscored by the concluding words of the heavenly oracle. His intimate association with God is stressed by the father-son relation which recalls the office of king; however, the emphasis on the Servant role far outweighs this aspect.[14]

That Jesus acknowledged his baptismal experience as setting the tone for his ministry is highlighted by Luke. Immediately after baptism, Jesus, "full of the Holy Spirit . . . was led by the Spirit . . . in the wilderness" of temptation (4:1f.). Then Jesus returns from the wilderness "in the power of the Spirit" (4:14), enters the synagogue at Nazareth, and declares the purpose of his mission in terms of the Servant of Isa. 61:1-2. This is the very paragraph that makes understandable the descent of the Spirit at his baptism. Jesus' description of his mission in terms of the Suffering Servant of Second Isaiah corroborates the interpretation that he understood the revelatory experience at his baptism to be an appointment to this task. In the remainder of his ministry Jesus followed this task.

Jesus sought out John. From a heart searching for expression he decided in favor of John's proclamation. God's presence was a reality, his kingdom was imminent, men must be willing to accept God's judgement. Jesus concretized and dramatized his decision in the act of baptism. Then came the fulfillment. The searching heart submitting totally to the will of God found its destiny in God's plan. A heart dedicated to God's demand was receptive to God's challenge—to a mission in God's service. All of this occurred in the context of the drama of baptism. The early church and the Gospel writers could not ignore the fact that for Jesus the decision for baptism and the understanding of his mission were inseparable.

Who Follows?

A comparison of the messages of John and Jesus discloses one certainty—both centered on the imminence of the kingdom of God. This is obvious from the previous discussion of John's message and from Jesus' sermon in Luke 4.[15] Matthew accents the continuity of Jesus' message with that of John's by quoting the same words from the lips of each: "Repent for the kingdom of heaven is at hand" (Mt. 3:2; 4:17). Yet the reader of the Gospels misses any reference in Jesus' preaching to baptism. If baptism were so crucial in Jesus' experience, why did he not call others to a similar experience? If others, through Jesus' preaching, decided for the kingdom, did he call them to dramatize their decision in baptism? If this was so important to John, and if Jesus continued his message, why did he not administer John's baptism also?

Some of Jesus' disciples had earlier experienced baptism at the hands of John. While their call to vocation differed they did make a decision in baptism similar to that of Jesus, i.e., they placed their lives under the judgement of God and his impending kingdom. They were associated with the movement of which they subsequently recognized Jesus as leader replacing John. When these disciples transfer their allegiance to Jesus (Jn. 1:35ff.), there would be no reason to re-baptize them.

Evidently Jesus did administer baptism, especially during the early part of his ministry. The first three Gospels have made no reference to Jesus' early Judean ministry; however, the Fourth Gospel gives us a glimpse into his initial activities. It describes a brief period of baptizing in Judea while John was baptizing near Aenon. Jesus' action is interpreted by some of John's disciples as competitive. This gives the Baptist an opportunity to give witness to the authenticity of Jesus. Now one thing seems certain: Jesus did baptize (Jn. 3:22, 26; 4:1). The later explanation that not Jesus but his disciples baptized (4:2) is most probably an editorial insertion to explain the problem that Jesus seemed to baptize at first but did not continue throughout his ministry.[16] This is even stranger to the modern reader, since the rite has become so important for Christians, although Jesus baptized only for a short time.

While the Fourth Gospel does not elaborate the setting of Jesus' baptismal activity, it must be assumed that it was in keeping with his message of the imminence of the kingdom of God, and that it was an expression of one's commitment to that kingdom. Baptism afforded the respondents to Jesus' proclamation an opportunity to dramatize their decision. Because Jesus patterns his earliest preaching after that of John, it might be expected that he would adopt John's baptism also. But beyond the brief reference in the Fourth Gospel, no source refers to Jesus' baptizing anyone again. This may be explained by his moving out of the area of the Jordan or by the fact that his ministry developed too swiftly to incorporate the rite. To discover the final reason why Jesus did not use baptism during his ministry or, if he did, why the Synoptic writers have failed to report it, is beyond the grasp of the modern interpreter.

§

In recording information about Jesus the Gospel writers give us hints of his life before his public ministry. As an inquisitive, sensitive person he had a searching heart. Considering diligently the possible options, Jesus found the declaration of John a challenge to his search. Affirming the authenticity of John's message, Jesus demonstrated his decision to be committed to God's call through the drama of baptism. In this context he became fully aware of his vocation as God's Servant-Son who would carry out God's will. His vocation included the preaching of repentance and for a brief period the practice of baptism.

In recording information about Jesus the Gospel writers have emphasized Jesus' association with baptism. He accepted the rite as appropriate for himself as well as for others. He led others to participate in it. Matthew further records that the risen Lord commanded his disciples to baptize successive generations of Christians:

> Go therefore and make disciples of all nations, baptizing them in the name of the Father and of the Son and of the Holy Spirit. (Mt. 28:19)

3
NOTES

1. See above, 4-6.
2. H. D. A. Major, T. W. Manson, C. J. Wright, *The Mission and Message of Jesus* (New York: E. P. Dutton, 1938), 271.
3. Ibid., 271f.
4. See above, 1-4.
5. See above, 7-11; cf. S. G. F. Brandon, *Jesus and the Zealots* (New York: Charles Scribner's Sons, 1967), for the development of the thesis that Jesus belonged to this militant party.
6. See above, 11-19.
7. Mt. 3:14f. has been regarded by some as an early Christian explanation of why the sinless Christ came to John's baptism. cf. F. W. Beare, *The Earliest Records of Jesus* (New York: Abingdon, 1962), 41; on the other hand, if our interpretation of repentance is correct, then Beare's explanation is not appropriate.
8. Bowman, *The Intention of Jesus*, 34.
9. Taylor, *Gospel*, 160; cf. 2 Baruch 22:1; T Levi 2:6; 5:1; 18:6; T Judah 24:2; Jn. 1:51; Acts 7:56; Rev. 4:1; 11:19; 19:11.
10. I. Abrahams, *Studies in Pharisaism and the Gospels* (Cambridge: At the University Press, 1917), first series, 47; Barrett, *Holy Spirit*, 38ff.; cf. H. L. Strack and P. Billerbeck, *Kommentar zum neuen Testament aus Talmud und Midrasch* (Munchen: C. H. Becksche Verlagsbuchhandlung, 1922-56), 1:123ff.
11. The point in this section is to emphasize the heavenly response to Jesus' baptismal experience rather than to determine an expanded theology of the presence of the Spirit in the earthly existence of Jesus.
12. See above, ch. 1.
13. Examine all the Servant Poems of Isaiah: 42:1-4; 49:1-6; 50:4-11; 52:13-53:12. Cf. Mowinckel, *He that Cometh*, 206-13, for the work of the Servant.
14. Cf. Taylor, *Gospel*, 162, for a significant discussion of this point.

15. See above, 13-19.

16. Cf. C. H. Dodd, *Historical Tradition in the Fourth Gospel*, (Cambridge: At the University Press, 1963), 279-97, for a discussion of Jesus' baptismal activity in these texts.

4 | *The Drama Continued*

The records of the earliest Christians describe their baptizing activity. Throughout the Book of Acts there are episodes in which baptism is an important part. Peter preaches and calls for baptism, Philip evangelizes and people are baptized, Paul propagates the gospel among the Gentiles and they request baptism. One thing seems quite certain: the earliest Christians practiced the rite of baptism.

From a New Motivation

Some disciples had been with Jesus throughout his earthly ministry and thus could give witness to the things they had heard and seen of Jesus. Yet there are times when the disciples are amazingly dense in understanding Jesus' purpose and mission. On one occasion Jesus chides his disciples: "Do you not yet understand?" (Mk. 8:21). Peter is reprimanded because he does not understand Jesus' prediction of the passion (Mk. 8:33). Other times they simply do not get the point (Mk. 9:32) or even distort the purpose that Jesus has in mind (Mk. 9:34; 10:37f.). The women did not expect to discover the empty tomb, for they brought spices to anoint the body of Jesus. One tradition even records Peter's distraction from the mission of Jesus to the extent that he returns to his fishing business (Jn. 21:3). Perhaps the most obvious misunderstanding was the disciples' concern for the reestablishment of the Davidic kingdom just before the ascension (Acts 1:6).

Dramatically, all this is changed. By the Day of Pentecost Peter is able to articulate a coherent interpretation of the meaning of

Jesus' life, death, and resurrection. The question must be asked: What made the difference? The early Christians were quite certain of the answer—the coming of the Holy Spirit. On the one hand, the disciples failed to comprehend Jesus' purpose and mission before Pentecost; on the other hand, the church after Pentecost does understand. The only possible explanation is the coming of the Holy Spirit. It became the animating force to the disciples' knowledge of the data of Jesus' words and deeds. It was the coming of the Spirit coupled with the disciples' past experiences with Jesus—his deeds, teaching, death, and resurrection—that gave rise to the proclamation of the gospel by the early disciples.

Now the coming of the Spirit was linked with the messianic era,[1] and its appearance on Jesus had been recorded by the Synoptic writers (Mk. 1:10). In addition to this Jesus promised the disciples the benefits of the Spirit during his lifetime. When he warns of persecution, he assures them that the Spirit of the Father will speak through them (Mt. 10:20). Finally the risen Lord commands his disciples to await the coming of the Spirit in Jerusalem, for its coming will mark the beginning of their testimony about him (Acts 1:5).

The coming of the Spirit is vividly described in Acts 2:1-4. This is the culmination of Jesus' promises to the disciples. So profound was the experience that the earliest Christians recognized it as the turning point in their understanding of Christ and their mission on his behalf. They could never forget it. Henceforth they were well aware that all that had been made known had come through the Spirit (1 Cor. 2:10; Gal. 2:8), which motivates them to share what they know about Jesus as Lord and Savior. For them the proclamation of John the Baptist that the one who would baptize with the Spirit was about to appear was indeed fulfilled.

In response to the coming of the Spirit Peter proclaims that the messianic era has begun in Jesus of Nazareth, whom God anointed to preach the good news of peace. This Jesus was crucified but resurrected from the dead. This became the church's new understanding of the role of Jesus in God's plan, and it gladly accepted its vital role in proclaiming this understanding.

The proclamation of the early Christians as set forth by Peter (1) began with the belief that *the time of fulfillment had dawned.*[2] The coming of the Spirit was one manifestation of this, for this was what the prophets had foreseen. So Joel 2:28-32 is quoted along with a general reference to all the prophets since Samuel (Acts 3:24). All that the prophets had hoped for was now being

realized. The beginning of the end-period was dawning. Peter
could declare with confidence:

> And in the last days it shall be, God declares,
> that I will pour out my Spirit upon all flesh. (Acts 2:17)

That is to say the early Christians grounded their proclamation
in the hope of the OT that God would visit his people with a
deliverance that would be recognized and accepted by all mankind.
They were not proclaiming some novel religious ideology. They
were not offering innovations to the older traditions; rather, they
were claiming that their proclamations were the proper fruition
of God's prior promises to mankind through Israel of old,
especially those made through her prophets. Thus Peter's very
first affirmation was that what was happening and what he had to
say was in direct continuity with the faith and hope of Israel.

The coming of the Spirit that provoked the immediate sermon
of Peter is a part of a larger event, namely the event of Jesus. So
the sermon continued: (2) *It was Jesus' ministry, death, and
resurrection that sparked the new era which was being attested by
the Spirit* (Acts 2:22-28). This was the second point in the
primitive proclamation. The early Christians placed Jesus and
specific features of his ministry in the very heart of their proclamation. Jesus' hometown was known—Nazareth. He had performed
mighty works—healing bodies and casting out demons. These
were signs that God was working through him (Acts 2:22; 10:38).
This very brief statement in Peter's sermon calls attention to the
importance the early Christians placed on Jesus' ministry as a
part of the salvation event which they were proclaiming. Furthermore, Jesus' life and death were significant as a part of God's
plan. God had intended from the beginning that Jesus would be
the central feature of his salvation. Even Jesus' ancestry attested
to his place of importance, for he was a descendant of David, i.e.,
God would set one of David's heirs on his throne (Acts 2:30). This
again welded the proclamation of salvation to the hope of the OT,
where the key figure in God's deliverance was usually described
as one of the Davidic house. But if Jesus' ministry was so
important, how could his death be explained? It too was a part of
God's salvation plan, for it was in accord with God's design that
Jesus was crucified. It was unthinkable that anything could have
happened to Jesus—the bringer of salvation—which was not
within God's plan. All of this shows that the earliest Christians
placed the historic Jesus in the center of their proclamation that

the new era was dawning. Without him there was no new era—no salvation from God.

The next emphasis in the early Christian proclamation was (3) *the resurrection of Jesus.* Through God's intervention death was not able to overcome the one whom he had appointed as the inaugurator of the new era. The very historic Jesus who had performed wonderful deeds as signs of God's approval was the one whom God raised. "This Jesus God raised up" (Acts 2:32). According to Peter's and the early church's understanding, this too, was grounded in the OT; it was part of God's plan; so it was fitting to quote Psalm 16:10 as applying to Jesus' resurrection. While the Christians gladly found OT quotations describing the importance of Jesus, they could do so because in their own experiences with Jesus they had witnessed the very thing toward which they believed the OT pointed. This was especially true of the resurrection—"of that we all are witnesses" (Acts 2:32; cf. 10:41). While countless numbers of people throughout Galilee witnessed the wonderful deeds performed by him, Jesus appeared to only a limited number of disciples after the resurrection. These appearances are described in the closing chapters of each of the Gospels, with further additions by Paul in 1 Corinthians 15. That the witnesses to the resurrection had a significant role in the early church is emphasized by the criteria used to select Judas' replacement in the band of the Twelve. The replacement must be one who had been with Jesus from the baptism of John until the day Jesus was taken up—"one of these men must become with us a witness to his resurrection" (Acts 1:22).

The resurrection was the vital center of the proclamation. Without it what had gone before, the wonderful deeds of Jesus and his teaching, even the crucifixion, would have had little relevance; without it the disciples would not have found themselves awaiting the coming of the Spirit which gave birth to their proclamation. Without the resurrection the early Christians could not have affirmed nor could Peter preach that (4) *Jesus had ascended to the very presence of God exalted to the position of prestige and authority at the right hand* (Acts 2:33). This was the position reserved for the Messiah. Thus, because of the resurrection, the proclamation climaxed in the assertion "God has made him both Lord and Christ, this Jesus whom you crucified" (Acts 2:36). He was the one ushering in the new era; he was the bringer of God's kingdom to mankind; he was the one opening the way of access to God's giving to humankind the possibility of a new life. This was what the early Christians were asserting in their proclamation.

The fifth emphasis returns to the matter of the Spirit, for the presence of (5) *the Holy Spirit* is not only a sign that the new era has dawned, but it *is also verification of the exaltation of Christ.* It is because of Christ's exaltation that the Spirit came upon the Christians at Pentecost (Acts 2:33). So the crucial significance of the coming of the Holy Spirit cannot be overemphasized. It was that moment or event which brought understanding to all that the disciples had previously experienced with and about Jesus and gave them the compulsion to articulate coherently the meaning of the life, death, and resurrection of Jesus.

In explaining the meaning of the gospel, Peter calls attention to the (6) *future consummation* of the new era which Jesus has inaugurated. In quoting Psalm 110:1, Peter is aware that Christ's function is not complete, for he will yet see victory over all the hostile forces of the world.

> The Lord said to my Lord, "Sit at my right hand,
> till I make thy enemies a stool for thy feet."
> (Acts 2:34f. = Ps. 110:1)

For the disciples the new era was dawning, but it was not yet complete. Peter again stresses the point when he speaks of

> Jesus, whom heaven must receive until the time for establishing all that God spoke by the mouth of his holy prophets from of old. (Acts 3:21)

Peter, like other early Christians, was steeped in the Jewish doctrine of the future which spoke in terms of a final eschaton (era) in which history and human affairs conformed to the purpose God had determined. This doctrine sometimes took the form of an anticipated judgement at the end of the present historical era when God's sovereignty would be apparent to all mankind. Different schemes of the attendant events were given. Sometimes the Messiah and his era preceded God's judgement, sometimes the Messiah participated in the judgement, sometimes only God was involved. Yet one thing was sure, God would overthrow the power of evil and judge against unrighteousness. The picture of the final judgement included the resurrection of the dead who would be judged and the righteous would be ushered into a new life.[3] The early Christians saw in Christ the purpose God had determined, but they did not yet see humanity conforming to that purpose. Thus, there must be a time out there in the future when the purpose of God in Christ would be completely realized.

Such an understanding would answer the question that, if Jesus was the Messiah, why had the glorious rule of God with the defeat of evil not yet appeared. For Peter it had begun. There were evidences of the power of God over evil in the mighty works of Jesus and in God's power to overcome the forces of death and raise Jesus from the dead. The new era was beginning, but not yet completely present. Furthermore, an understanding which saw the beginning and looked forward to the end of the Messianic era accounted for Jesus' own statements about the future. It cannot be overlooked that Jesus thought in terms of a future event when God's sovereignty would be manifest. Especially is this obvious in such statements as: "and you shall see the Son of Man at the right hand of Power, and coming with the clouds of heaven" (Mk. 14:62). That the future was a topic of conversation between Jesus and his disciples is attested by Mark 13.[4] Because the early church believed that Jesus was the Messiah and that he taught about the future, and because they were convinced that the resurrection declared God's victory over the forces of evil, they could look forward to the future consummation of the power of God when all would recognize Jesus as the true Messiah. So Peter could declare:

> And he commanded us to preach to the people, and to testify
> that he is the one ordained by God to be judge of the living and
> the dead. (Acts 10:42)

The earliest Christian sermons, and specifically the one by Peter on the Day of Pentecost, emphasized the six points described above. Such a proclamation had continuity with both the message of John the Baptist and Jesus. John had declared that the kingdom of God was imminent with its messianic figure. Peter was declaring that the new era, i.e., the kingdom of God, was already operative; it was already set in motion. Jesus declared that the kingdom of God was present in his ministry. Peter reiterated that Jesus ushered in the new era. Yet Peter went beyond John in that he clearly identified the messianic figure with Jesus of Nazareth and made him the center of all his proclamation. While Peter did not necessarily go beyond Jesus of Nazareth, he certainly boldly proclaimed the messiahship of Jesus. What was sometimes veiled in the signs, parables, and sayings of Jesus, Peter now affirmed openly. All of this was done because the Holy Spirit intervened at Pentecost.

What was expected of those who heard such a proclamation? Repent! (Acts 2:38) John the Baptist demanded it. Jesus called for repentance, now Peter. If there is continuity in content between these three, there is also continuity in the demanded response. The response must be an affirmation of the validity of the challenge presented by the herald. Peter has spoken of Jesus the Messiah. How are the people to respond? They are to accept his challenge, they are to accept the authenticity of the message. This is what repentance means. The definition of repentance must be recalled: *"a call to make a moral decision between two alternative courses set before one."* In other words Peter is calling for a decision.

Now like his predecessor, *Peter also called for baptism.* John the Baptist demanded this as a drama of the decision made by those responding to his message. There is evidence that Jesus practiced the rite for a period of time. Peter was following the precedent set by them. He, too, called for some outward expression of one's inner decision. He is asking that those willing to accept his proclamation dramatize their acceptance in the act of baptism. Acts 2:41 simply notes that some were baptized. While the texts made it quite clear that John baptized in the Jordan, the details of the circumstances of Peter's baptismal activity in Jerusalem are not given.

Peter described the kind of baptism which he requested as being in "the name of Jesus Christ" (Acts 2:38). That is to say there was no mistake about the frame of reference in which the drama was set; it was clearly a baptism in reference to Jesus. This is only fitting since all of Peter's sermon centered on the place of Jesus in God's activity. Jesus, the Messiah, is now the new avenue of approach to God, thus any overt symbol of one's decision toward Jesus will be made on his behalf. So Peter can speak of baptism in Jesus' name.[5] Furthermore, this repentance—decision articulated in baptism—has a reference to the forgiveness of sins.[6] Peter's sermon created a sense of guilt in those who are willing to respond. They had let Jesus pass through their very midst during his earthly ministry and had not responded to him, and perhaps they felt some corporate responsibility for his death. In addition they may very well have been sensitive to the fact that they had not been genuinely concerned for God and his kingdom. Already the decision to repentance was a confession that their relation to God was not a satisfactory one and a recognition of their own need. It is in this sense that the decision and baptism fits into the same context as forgiveness which is the removal of the guilt that has resulted from the previous erroneous stance before God. A decision for Christ properly orients one before God and at the same time God removes the stigma of any prior sins. This is forgiveness.

In addition to forgiveness Peter promises the gift of the Holy Spirit. Having begun his sermon with a quotation from Joel's description of the last days, when God would pour out his Spirit on all flesh, and having related the manifestation of the Spirit just prior to his sermon to the exaltation of Christ, he then assures his listeners that this blessing is available to all who decide in favor of the new era ushered in by Christ. It will be the verification in their own experience that they are entering the new era of the fulfillment of God's promises.

Peter's presentation ended where it began, with the Holy Spirit. It was out of the motivating force of the Spirit that Peter was able to understand clearly and articulate coherently the meaning of Jesus' role in God's plan. He boldly proclaimed this to those in Jerusalem on the Day of Pentecost. He concluded his proclamation with a demand for a decision dramatized in the act of baptism and a promise of the Holy Spirit. This new motivation moved the early church to other opportunities for proclamation.

Further Proclamation

Peter's dramatic sermon on the Day of Pentecost was only the beginning of his activities as a herald of the good news of God's new era in Christ. Daily he entered the temple witnessing to his Lord (Acts 2:46ff.). He became the chief spokesman for the Jerusalem church, and as a result of his preaching many were added to the fellowship (Acts 2:47). Although the author of Acts does not mention baptism every time he notes the increase of the church, it must be assumed that the new converts were confronted by the same proclamation that Peter had preached on the Day of Pentecost including the challenge to express their positive decision in the outward act of baptism.

In addition to Jerusalem, Peter's travels in Palestine took him to the villages of Samaria where he proclaimed the gospel (Acts 8:14ff.). He also traveled to Lydda, Sharon, and finally came to Joppa (Acts 9:32ff.). It was at Joppa that *Peter received the vision preparing him for the invitation from Cornelius* to come to his residence in Caesarea for the purpose of explaining the gospel to him. Cornelius was already familiar with the basic tenets of the Jewish faith. He is described as a "God-fearing man" who had a worthy reputation among the Jewish people (Acts 10:22). This probably means that he was a patron of the Jewish synagogue in Caesarea where he participated as an associate member.[7] He was well acquainted with the Jewish teachings and had a profound respect for their ancient monotheistic tradition and their high moral standards. There would be no reason to doubt that he was aware of the main tenets of Jewish eschatology including the hope of the Messiah, the resurrection, and the judgement. He knew completely the route he must follow if he chose to become fully accepted as a synagogue member: circumcision, baptism, sacrifice. He could not forget the embarrassment he would suffer from his Roman friends and even ostracism if he should totally embrace Judaism, for to do so he must become a Jew.

This may be the point at which he became interested in Peter's proclamation, for it was introduced by an OT prophecy which looked forward to a time when *all* peoples would be included in God's favor, not just Jews. As one standing outside the Jewish heritage looking in, Cornelius would have been more open to the universal implications of Peter's new proclamation than perhaps Peter himself. Because of his acquaintance with and appreciation for the Jewish faith he wished to hear more about this newer interpretation that declared a universal Messiah. So he invited Peter to his residence.

When Peter arrived there were, of course, explanatory remarks regarding the occasion; but Peter soon began to set forth his understanding of Jesus. It was Jesus of Nazareth whom God anointed to preach the good news to Israel. This he did throughout Galilee and Judea. His life ended in execution, but God raised him up on the third day. Of all of this Peter and others are witnesses. Peter is here restating what he has stated before—God has begun something new in the life, death, and resurrection of Jesus. This is the idea of the new era. Peter stresses Jesus' place in the messianic era by noting that God has designated him the judge at the appointed hour (Acts 10:42). From the beginning of the sermon Peter opened the door for a positive response on the part of Cornelius. He affirms that God will accept anyone, from any nation, "who fears him and does what is right" (Acts 10:34). In this speech Peter's call for decision is not conveyed in a call for repentance but in the promise that "everyone who believes in him receives forgiveness of sins through his name" (Acts 10:43). Here the response of believing is comparable to the call for repentance in his earlier sermon. The one who believes enjoys the forgiveness elaborated in the discussion of Peter's previous sermon. Peter does not have the opportunity to explain the role of the Spirit, for it descends upon the group before he can finish. The coming of the Spirit was evidence that Cornelius and his group had made a positive decision to Peter's proclamation. Thus Peter could call for their overt action witnessing to that response. He commands them "to be baptized in the name of Jesus Christ" (Acts 10:48). This act was the proper culmination of the process of proclamation and response, for it vividly dramatized the decision for the gospel made by the participants.

This is the other main incident recorded in Acts, in addition to Pentecost, where Peter's proclamation culminates in baptism; but these two, along with the other references which will be mentioned, have been presented by the author of Acts in order to show the pattern of baptism in the early church. It is quite obvious from a study of Acts that baptism was the normal rite for entering the fellowship of the church.[8] What is more important is that the rite comes to those who have made a favorable decision for the gospel as an outward expression of that decision.

Earlier, however, Peter was involved in an anticlimactic way with Philip's preaching in *the district of Samaria*. Actually the story of Philip's leaving Jerusalem after the martyrdom of Stephen to preach the gospel elsewhere is the first account of preaching beyond Jerusalem told by the author of Acts (8:4–13). When he arrived in one of the Samaritan towns, Philip proclaimed the Messiah. They would understand this, for they had their own doctrine of the Messiah. The Samaritan woman to whom Jesus spoke at Jacob's well acknowledged her interest in the Messiah (John 4:25, 29). The Samaritans shared the teaching of the Pentateuch with the Jews and so did not represent a totally different religious orientation to what the disciples were accustomed. Philip's proclamation of the Messiah was not strange to them; and, as it was accompanied by many signs, there is no surprise that many responded. Philip's preaching also included the kingdom of God and the name of Jesus Christ. His proclamation continued in the tradition begun by John the Baptist and developed by Jesus. While the text of his message is not given in detail, it was the intention of the author of Acts to show that he was continuing the mainstream of the gospel as enunciated by Peter at Pentecost.

As the people heard and believed, they were baptized. A full description of the process of baptism is not given. The occasion must, however, be interpreted along the lines of Peter's Pentecost sermon where there was a specific challenge to repentance, forgiveness, and baptism. It was because of their accepting Philip's claim about the reality of the kingdom, God's presence with them, and the authenticity of Jesus' role as Messiah that they were baptized. They were expressing their decision in favor of Philip's proclamation.

Now the author of Acts felt no difficulty in reporting that the Holy Spirit did not come upon the Samaritan disciples until Peter and John arrived from Jerusalem. Luke simply reported the material he found about the Samaritan church. Yet he could not have been insensitive to the fact that this episode was different from the Pentecost experience in Jerusalem and the coming of the Spirit upon Cornelius in Caesarea. In both cases the Spirit came spontaneously, not with the laying on of hands. The reader might wonder whether Luke was trying to establish some principle whereby the Spirit could not be granted until the laying on of hands by an apostle. If so, he has missed an opportunity to make the point by controlling the data about Peter's visit to Cornelius where it would have been quite simple to report the matter as if the Spirit came at Peter's discretion rather than spontaneously. Evidently, Luke is more interested in reporting the experiences of the early church than establishing a rigid model for the blessing of the Spirit.

Why then did it happen that the Spirit did not come until after the arrival of Peter and John? Did they have the privilege of being religious inspectors? No doubt the early church in Jerusalem was interested in verifying the authenticity of the religious experiences of the Christians in new situations. Another case where this is implied is when Barnabas was sent to Antioch in Syria (Acts 11:22). This would be an occasion of sharing joy and mutual encouragement rather than a formal inspection. So Peter and John came for mutual edification. To ask the question whether a church could exist without the outpouring of the Spirit is to subject the experiences of primitive Christians to more refined theological formulations than they had need. The early Christians were groping for patterns, not operating on well-established rules. Obviously the Samaritan Christians had already experienced a great deal of joy because of the signs of the presence of the kingdom and the name of Christ (vv. 8, 12). This would certainly imply some working of the Spirit in Philip's activity.[9] Peter and John simply desired that the new converts experience the more pronounced manifestation of the Spirit comparable to that in Jerusalem at Pentecost and in Caesarea at Cornelius' house. It is not a totally satisfying suggestion that Peter's and John's laying on of hands represented the granting of spiritual gifts,[10] although Simon may have understood that some magical powers were being transmitted (Acts 8:19). One thing is obvious: Luke is emphasizing that the presence of the Spirit was a reality for those who decided in favor of the proclamation of God's nearness in Christ. For those who opted for the kingdom there was the abiding assurance of God's presence.

In the stories of chapters 8 and 9 of Acts the author is telling how Christianity spread from Jerusalem in various directions after the persecution following Stephen's martyrdom. It moves to Samaria, then toward the south, and finally in chapter 9 it confronts Paul en route to Damascus. Luke includes the story of the Ethiopian eunuch to note the gospel's ever expanding circumference to embrace all men, but in doing so he has given the reader another scene of baptism.

The story moves swiftly and the details are few. In a compressed account *Philip meets the eunuch*, joins him in the chariot, expounds Isaiah 53:7-8 to him, preaches the good news of Jesus, baptizes him, and departs his company. The key sentence describing Philip's response to the eunuch is: "and beginning with this scripture he told him the good news of Jesus" (8:35). This Servant passage from Isaiah is frequently applied to Jesus in the NT;[11] at this point Luke assumes his readers will understand how Philip interpreted the passage. Furthermore, the author is not obligated to elaborate on "the good news of Jesus" since he carefully articulated Peter's Pentecost sermon. The reader knows that this includes the declaration that the kingdom of God is present with its promises and blessings, that the Holy Spirit is operative, that Jesus is the inaugurator of the messianic era, and that man is to repent and be baptized in response to this proclamation. That the eunuch understood this is obvious from his reaction. He wishes to record his decision in favor of Philip's proclamation by being baptized. Whether the eunuch had met the new ideas before or confronted them for the first time with Philip,[12] one thing is certain—he was determined to declare his acceptance of the "good news." His question, "What is to prevent my being baptized?" may very well reflect the hindrances he had met in worshipping at

Jerusalem; for, being a eunuch, he was restrained by priestly law from becoming a full participant in Jewish ceremonies (Dt. 23:1). The question also expresses his joy that he can be included in the blessings of God because the messianic era has begun for all men in the coming of Jesus. Since the Spirit has been poured out on all flesh (Acts 2:16ff.), what could possibly hinder even this eunuch from full participation? He is eager to dramatize his involvement with the Messiah. He has heard the proclamation, he accepts it. He asks for baptism, he dramatizes his decision.

In this baptism episode no reference is made specifically to the coming of the Spirit upon the baptized, neither immediately as in the case of the Pentecost experience and Cornelius, nor later as in the case of the Samaritans. Yet surely Philip had included in his exposition of the good news—and certainly the eunuch had understood as part of the promise—the coming of the Spirit. That the Spirit was operative in the entire episode is stressed by the fact that as they came up out of the water the Spirit whisked Philip away and the eunuch "went on his way rejoicing" (8:39)—a sign of the presence of the Spirit. Luke has not felt it necessary to explain the details, but he has said enough for the reader to understand that in the total experience the eunuch had found a new dimension to life. Evidently Luke was not consciously articulating a doctrine of baptism; yet by recording these narratives in their simple, compact form, he provided a significant insight into the meaning of that rite.[13]

The narratives of the *conversion of Saul* are the most dramatic of any description of the change the new era brought in a person's life. So decisive was the experience that Luke permits the story to be retold three times (Acts 9:1-8; 22:3-16; 26:9-20). The first time he tells the story as a part of the moving of Christianity away from Jerusalem: Philip goes toward Gaza, the eunuch is baptized; Peter goes to Caesarea, Cornelius is baptized; Saul journeys to Damascus, he is baptized.

In each of the stories of his conversion, Saul is portrayed as one eager to destroy the young sectarian group which is preaching that Jesus is the Messiah and challenging people to repent and be baptized. He is fully aware of their proclamation. There is no uncertainty in his mind about the error of their message. It must be ended. He had dedicated himself to the eradication of this movement. In such a frame of mind, as Saul neared Damascus, the miracle took place. In a strange, mysterious way the risen Lord confronted Saul and identified himself as Jesus of Nazareth (22:8)—the very thing Saul resented most.

In this experience, Saul is convinced that Jesus of Nazareth was truly resurrected as proclaimed by Peter and others, for the resurrected one is appearing to him (1 Cor. 15:8). So Saul can, without reservation, identify Jesus with the true Messiah of Israel. The persecutor of Christ is in effect deciding in favor of Christ; he comes to the disturbing conclusion that what he was formerly seeking to destroy is in actuality the very truth for which he longed. Jesus is the Christ—the messianic age has dawned—the decision is made—he will participate.

Saul is blind and unable to take food for three days. Ananias of Damascus ministers to him and he is restored. Ananias understands that his ministry to Saul is to offer the Holy Spirit and baptism. He says that "Jesus . . . has sent me that you may . . . be filled with the Holy Spirit" (Acts 9:17). While the actual experience of his receiving the Spirit is not described, Saul takes up the very task of those who first received the Spirit on Pentecost: "he proclaimed Jesus, saying, 'He is the Son of God'" (Acts 9:20). There can be no doubt that Saul was genuinely filled with the Spirit.

Having been filled with the Spirit and prior to his public proclamation, Saul was baptized (Acts 9:18). His own story of the experience in Acts 22 clarifies the matter somewhat. Saul, now called Paul, credits Ananias with the articulation of God's call for him to be a witness to all men. Then Ananias adds "and now why do you wait? Rise and be baptized, and wash away your sins, calling on his name" (Acts 22:16). The entire experience of coming to the conclusion that Jesus is the Messiah, receiving the Holy Spirit, appointed as a witness, culminated in the act of baptism.

Paul knew well what baptism meant. He was well schooled in the use of water ablutions in Judaism and understood the ritual of proselyte baptism. He knew that such a rite was predicated upon a decision in favor of a new course of life. There was some embarrassment, some stigma, for a devout rabbi, a Pharisee, to be baptized; yet, for one who had so dramatically decided in favor of a new course of life, why should he hesitate to dramatize his decision openly? Had not the disciples of John done this? Had not other converts participated? So Paul, too, was baptized and indelibly associated himself with those who were proclaiming Jesus as the Christ.

Ananias' admonition to "get your sins washed away" is a further reference to the drama of baptism. It stands in the same frame of reference as Peter's remark: "Repent . . . be baptized . . .

for the forgiveness of sins."[14] For just as baptism was the drama of Paul's decision for Christ it was also the drama that Paul had been accepted. His sins were forgiven, the inner guilt of his conduct against Christ was removed. Paul's prior opposition to God and refusal to accept the Messiah not only changed, but the alienation between Paul and God was overcome. His sins were washed away. For one well versed in the Jewish Scriptures, washing appropriately symbolized the removal of sin and guilt:

> Wash yourselves; make yourselves clean;
>   remove the evil of your doings from before my eyes;
> cease to do evil, learn to do good. (Isa. 1:16f.)

> Wash me thoroughly from my iniquity,
>   and cleanse me from my sin! (Ps. 51:2)

Ananias chose a fitting way to describe baptism: it dramatized not only the decision, but the removal of guilt and the restoration of a proper fellowship as well. All of this was done while calling upon the name of the Lord (Acts 22:16).[15]

That the Apostle Paul took the rite of baptism seriously is attested by the fact that he practiced it on his journeys. During Paul's missionary activity in the city of Philippi, Luke records two baptisms. Paul meets Lydia by the riverside (Acts 16:14ff.). It is said that "The Lord opened her heart to give heed to what was said by Paul," signifying her positive response to what Paul proclaimed. An example of Paul's proclamation is given by Luke in Acts 13:16-41 where the basic content recalls Peter's sermon in Acts 2. That is to say Paul's proclamation was in keeping with that of the early church, and it would follow that the response should be baptism. Lydia and her household were baptized.

Another case of the apostle's baptismal activities in Philippi is the jailer. Since the writer of Acts had already made known the content of the apostolic preaching (2:14-41) and Paul's agreement with it, it was not necessary for him to repeat Paul's full explanation to the jailer. The succinct invitation was "Believe in the Lord Jesus, and you will be saved" (16:31). The jailer's response to Paul's invitation was first to minister unto Paul's physical needs, for Paul and Silas had been beaten by the guards. Afterwards the jailer was baptized. He was demonstrating his response. He made it obvious that he was totally involved in what the apostle had explained.

That Paul's ministry, a part of the earliest Christian history, included the practice of baptism is further attested by his experience in Corinth, where, after being expelled from the synagogue for preaching that the Christ was Jesus, many of the people believed and were baptized (Acts 18:8). Again, Luke has not given the total preachment of Paul nor a detailed statement of the response of the people. Simply, Paul preached that Jesus is Christ; the people believed; they were baptized. Of course, the record of Paul's preaching to the Corinthians is preserved in his epistles addressed to that church. Especially in 1 Corinthians 2, Paul reiterates that the focal point of his preaching was Jesus Christ who was crucified (1 Cor. 2:2), and how the corroboration of the Spirit was a part of God's blessing to them (1 Cor. 2:10).

This epistle further calls attention to the baptismal activity of Paul when he admits that he baptized the household of Stephanas and maybe others he has forgotten (1 Cor. 1:16). It is beside the point whether Paul was the actual administrant of the rite of baptism in Corinth. The important point is that he preached; people responded; they believed; they were baptized. They were accepting baptism as a meaningful expression of their faith-response to the message preached by Paul.

Now the question must be asked whether or not infants were included in these baptismal ceremonies. Four times the book of Acts has a summary reference to a household's being baptized. The first incident is in the home of Cornelius at Caesarea (Acts 10:23-48). When Peter is summarizing this episode to his colleagues in Jerusalem, he describes Cornelius as one seeking him who has a message by which he will be saved "and all your household" (Acts 11:14). The group to whom Peter preaches when he goes to Caesarea is described as Cornelius' "kinsmen and close friends" (10:24). As Peter proclaimed the gospel to them, "the Holy Spirit fell on all who heard the word" (v. 44). Then they were baptized. The group gathered by Cornelius is not a household group made up of children and slaves, but rather those associates of his who have similar interest in understanding the proclamation of this new Jewish Messiah. Further, those who are baptized are those "who heard the word." Nothing in this context suggests the presence of children; rather, the situation strongly implies a group of people seeking the truth. When they heard, they were capable of responding, for they spoke in tongues as the disciples had done on the Day of Pentecost. There is no reason to suppose children were present; rather, any implication strongly suggests only persons of a responsible age.[16]

The second episode in Acts that might raise a question about infant baptism is the case of Lydia in Philippi (Acts 16:11-15).

After God opened her heart to receive the gospel, "she was baptized, with her household" (v. 15). In the story all of the information centers around Lydia and the women; her vocation is described and her home background is given. This seems to exclude the presence of a husband.[17] Who then were in "her household"? The best suggestion would be those associated with her as assistants in her vocational pursuits: bond-servants or slaves, hired assistants, business associates. The scene of Paul's preaching to her is at a place of worship. She and those with her were already searching through their worship ceremonies for understanding. They were already of similar minds. Thus again there is no implication that children are present to receive baptism.

In the case of the Philippian jailer, the content of Acts 16:30-34 should be examined closely. When the jailer asks what he must do to be saved, the apostle's answer is certain: "Believe!" Verse 31 should be interpreted not that by the jailer's belief everyone would be saved, but rather that everyone in his house that believed would be saved.[18] To interpret the verse in the former way would be contrary to every other episode involving baptism which follows belief. That v. 31 should be explained this way is corroborated by v. 32 where the apostles speak "the word" to everyone in the house. The proclamation was made to the group, not just the jailer. As a result of the proclamation, those in the jailer's house were baptized. The stress of this episode, when properly interpreted, is on the response to the proclamation rather than the inclusion by parental decision of the infants of a household. The detailed makeup of those belonging to the jailer's household is not given.

One other reference may be mentioned. In Acts 18:8 Crispus "believed in the Lord, together with his household; and many of the Corinthians hearing Paul believed and were baptized." Again, any reading of this statement cannot ignore the emphasis on believing prior to the experience of baptism. There seems to be no remote allusion to infants being baptized.[19]

As the early Christians were caught by a new motivating force—the Holy Spirit—they fervently proclaimed the good news of God's salvation in Christ. Wherever this proclamation was set forth it called for acceptance, repentance, faith—not a limited, veiled, response, but a response dramatically portrayed by the believer. The proclamation demanded that those seriously deciding in favor of it should dramatize that decision in the act of baptism. Wherever people are baptized in the early church, as recorded in the NT, it is in response to the proclamation; the participant has heard; he believes; he is baptized. The early Christians demanded baptism because they knew that their Lord not only himself responded to God in the act of baptism, but he also commanded his disciples to practice it—a command that was authenticated by the resurrected Savior:

> All authority on heaven and in earth has been given to me. Go therefore and make disciples of all nations, baptizing them in the name of the Father and of the Son and of the Holy Spirit, teaching them to observe all that I have commanded you; and lo, I am with you always, to the close of the age.
>
> (Mt. 28:18b-20)

A Drama of Decision

For the early Christians there was no question about the decision they were making. They decided in favor of Jesus, God's promised Messiah. Because he had come they could participate in the new era, already begun with the expected completion in God's own good time. This was verified by Jesus' resurrection, ascension, and the coming of the Holy Spirit. These new converts were opting for a style of life that recognized God's nearness and abiding presence through what Jesus accomplished. They deliberately turned from whatever previous style of life they embraced to a Jesus style of life—they repented—they entered the kingdom.

For those who responded to the preaching of the early evangelists there was no mistake that Jesus was at the center of the message. Whatever the evangelists had to offer was because of Jesus. Any response to the evangelists would find it necessary to make a decision about Jesus. Was he or was he not the Messiah, the bringer of salvation? The decision was for or against Jesus. Baptism as the drama of the convert's decision is understood as an act inextricably associated with Jesus. At the close of Peter's first sermon he appeals to his hearers to "be baptized . . . in the name of Jesus Christ" (Acts 2:38). Peter did not alter his requirement when he preached to Cornelius, for "he commanded them to be baptized in the name of Jesus Christ" (Acts 10:48). In preaching to the Samaritans, Philip does not use the phrase "baptize in the name of Jesus," yet it is only after he has preached "the name of Jesus Christ" that the Samaritans respond and are baptized (Acts 8:12). Or again the eunuch is baptized after "the good news of Jesus" is preached to him (Acts 8:35). Paul, after his conversion, is ordered to be baptized, "calling on his name" (Acts 22:16). All of this is to point out that these early evangelists recognized that the significance of baptism depended upon Jesus Christ.

It has already been noted that the act of baptism is a drama declaring the convert's decision on behalf of the good news from God. *This baptismal formula "in the name of . . ." makes quite clear that the one dramatizing his decision is also portraying his intimate association with Christ.* This is what it means to "be baptized in the name of Jesus Christ."

On first reading one's analytical mind might suggest that the formula "in the *name* of Jesus Christ" is an effort to separate the essence of the person designated by the proper title Jesus Christ from some other aspect referred to by the word *name*. A name is much more than a mere reference to a person. It "is an indispensable part of the personality."[20] The name makes known who the person really is and in some mysterious way releases the energy or force latent within him.[21] The name also implies the reputation and status of the person. Such explanations may help in understanding the early Christian baptismal formula.

Further help is gained in understanding how one can perform an act in the name of another person by noting how the phrase was used in other contexts. Business documents from Egypt, written in Greek, are helpful. In these papyri texts the phrase "in the name of" has a legal reference. Documents authorizing legal action or responsibility are deposited with the appropriate authority "in the name of" the person concerned.[22] In the banking business deposits were made "in the name of" a person. It is even noted in a writing from Asia Minor that a citizen had made a purchase "in the name of" his god.[23]

The rabbis of the NT period used the phrase "in the name of" to mean "in virtue of the name," "on the basis of the name" "with appeal to the name of." An illustration of this would be that one might heal in the name of a distinguished person.[24] Here the status, virtue, or power of the person is emphasized. A further illustration from rabbinical literature would be the case of a Jewish slave who is being freed. He takes a ritual bath "in the name of a free man" to dramatize his freedom. Also proselytes accept circumcision "in the name of the covenant."[25] Thus he is received into the covenant fellowship.

These illustrations make it clear that to act in behalf of another or with reference to another's status or even a change in one's own status could be designated by "in the name of." When the name of deity was involved the matter was exceedingly serious. The Jews of Jesus' day would not utter the scriptural name for God— Yahweh. They substituted the word "Lord" or simply "the name." [26] The second commandment requires that "You shall not take the name of the Lord your God in vain." This was a demand that the people not enter an intimate relation with God without a deliberate decision to be true to their responsibilities. This was a prohibition against taking things pertaining to God with any degree of levity. Surely some degree of awe and reverence was involved when the Christian convert was "baptized in the name of Jesus Christ."

What then did it mean for one to be baptized "in the name of Jesus Christ?" It meant that the individual had heard the proclamation of the good news that salvation was present. He carefully, with awe and reverence, made a calculated decision in favor of the message. He willingly accepted the rite of baptism because it dramatized that he, the convert, was entering a new relationship with Christ based on Christ's status as the bringer of the new era and his essential reputation as verified by God. For the convert, baptism dramatized his movement from some other sphere of commitment to the sphere of Christ. He identified with the very person of Christ. He belonged to Christ.

But why did the early Christian choose the rite of baptism to dramatize this decision? It has already been discussed how baptism emerged out of the religious heritage of the Jews.[27] Whatever the reasons for the popularity of this rite in the first-century Palestine, one thing is certain: Jesus had been baptized in the Jordan River by John the Baptist. Here was reason enough for his disciples to be baptized and to baptize others. If the one bringing salvation, the new era, began his public career by being baptized, how fitting for his disciples to follow his example. Furthermore, Jesus himself had seen fit to relate to his disciples the importance of his baptismal experience. It was the dramatization of his unreserved commitment to the will of God. From that moment on he was in God's hands. The early Christians could share this. As Jesus was baptized as a sign of his commitment to the will of God so they too were baptized as a sign of their commitment to Jesus Christ— in his name. Because Jesus was baptized, the early Christians were baptized and required baptism of other new converts.

Accompanying this example of Jesus' own action was his command to make disciples, baptizing them. This terse imperative is recorded in Mt. 28:18b–20 and has been quoted above. This command is set in the framework of a post-resurrectional appearance of Jesus to his disciples, thus adding to its authority: "All authority in heaven and on earth has been given to me" (v. 18b). This statement may have in its background an allusion to Dan. 7:13f., where the Son of Man is given dominion over all nations. But the point is obvious, the resurrected Lord declares an authority beyond that which he enjoyed before his death. He now holds the dominion over which Satan bargained with him in the period of temptation. This authority is that to which Peter referred in his first Christian sermon where he noted that the resurrection verified Jesus' status. So it is the risen Lord, endowed with complete authority, who issues the command to his disciples.

The imperative Jesus issues is "to make disciples of all nations." The making of disciples was an integral part of Jesus' mission. People in general crowded to him and frequently he challenged individuals such as Peter, James, and John to follow him. Jesus also gave general invitations: "If anyone comes to me . . ." (Lk. 14:26). On two different occasions during his lifetime Jesus sent out his disciples to preach and heal. Furthermore, it has been argued that Jesus' intention was to bring into existence ideal Israel who would fulfill the destiny designed for her as described in the prophetic writings, especially Second Isaiah.[28] In his inaugural address, as recorded by Luke (ch. 4), Jesus associated himself with the thought of Second Isaiah. In the thought of this prophet the potential of Judaism to a world-wide mission reaches its highest expression. That is to say, although Jesus in his earthly mission made no effort to travel world-wide, there was inherent in his association with Second Isaiah the potential of a world mission. Now in his status of authenticated Son of Man he commands his disciples to the task.

The coming into existence of the apostles with their activity as evangelists is further verification of the missionary command of the risen Lord.[29] Their encounter with the resurrected Jesus and his commissioning of them to an evangelistic mission was the primary reason for the existence of the office of apostle.[30] If Jesus had intended his mission to continue after his departure, it is not only reasonable to suppose that those closest to him should continue the effort, but also likely that he would directly commission them to carry on what he had begun. At Jesus' death the disciples, who later became apostles, were afraid and disorganized. "The Gospels and Acts make it quite clear that it was exclusively the act of the risen Lord that this scattered group became a community full of hope and ready for action."[31] Why else would the apostles risk their very lives to accomplish the task of evangelism if they were not certain that they were acting under the commission of the risen, empowered, Lord?[32] The sharing of the proclamation about Jesus in such a way to lead others to be his disciples became the guiding aim of the early Christians.

Making disciples implies at least two corollaries: (1) commitment on the part of the disciples and (2) a body of ideas which the teacher imparts to the follower. The risen Lord's command to the apostles included both. It has already been shown that the disciples who committed themselves to the apostolic proclamation dramatized their decision in the rite of baptism. Why? Because Jesus had included it in his command to the apostles. There was no question in the mind of the early Christians that their practice of baptism was the intention of Jesus.[33] Because of his status and his intention it was appropriate to baptize in his name. It was a confession that the individual had been "discipled" to Jesus Christ. Jesus had been baptized by John in the Jordan River as a drama of his decision to submit to the will of God. He had either baptized others (John 3:22) or had approved his disciples' doing it (John 4:2) during his earthly ministry. In his commission to his apostles he commands its practice as a drama of commitment to discipleship.

The second corollary of Jesus' commission was that of teaching all that he had taught his disciples. Throughout his lifetime he was known as a teacher. The content of his teaching centered in the theme of the kingdom of God. This was the crucial issue to be faced—the kingdom and how to relate to it. Jesus had given much guidance in this matter. If his teachings were valid, they must be spread abroad. By confronting his teachings one could decide whether to become a serious disciple of Jesus and to demonstrate that commitment in the act of baptism.

It could be argued that the period of time the disciples spent in Jerusalem in semi-seclusion after the ascension was a period of recalling and assimilating the things the Lord had taught them.[34] They were "doing their homework" in preparation for the execution of the commission they had received from Jesus. That is to say, they were preparing for the teaching aspect of their mission. They began immediately to assemble the materials which Jesus had taught.

§

The apostles, as this chapter has shown, carried out the command of the risen Christ; they "discipled" others by proclaiming the good news about Christ; they baptized them as a drama of their decision; they further taught them what he had taught.

Baptism was an essential part of the life of the earliest Christians. They practiced it because Jesus had set the example, because the risen Christ had commanded it, and it vividly dramatized their decision in favor of the lordship of Christ in their lives. He had the status to give them a new status. He had the power to bring them into a new style of life—a new stance before God. Baptism was for the early Christian a drama of decision.[35]

4
NOTES

1. See above, 16-18.

2. The following discussion of early Christian proclamation is based on C. H. Dodd, *The Apostolic Preaching and its Developments* (London: Hodder and Stoughton, Ltd., 1936).

3. For the idea of the coming of the Messiah and the judgement, cf. Moore, *Judaism*, vol. 2, part 7; Mowinckel, *He that Cometh*, part 2; H. H. Rowley, *The Relevance of Apocalyptic* (London: Lutterworth Press, 1944), ch. 2. For a popular treatment of this idea see J. Bonsirven, *Palestinian Judaism in the Time of Christ*, transl. W. Wolf (New York: Holt, Rinehart, and Winston, 1964), chs. 8-10.

4. While Mark 13 has been the subject of much critical discussion among NT scholars, there is no question that Jesus did discuss the future. Cf. Taylor, *Gospel*. For a survey of the literature on this subject cf. G. R. Beasley-Murray, *Jesus and the Future* (London: Macmillan, 1954), esp. 172ff., for the author's conclusion in favor of the authenticity of Mark 13.

5. The phrase, "in the name of . . ." will be discussed later in this chapter; see below, 63-65.

6. The interpretation of Acts 2:38 hinges on the prepositional phrase translated in the RSV "for the forgiveness of your sins" with the focus being on the preposition translated "for." Regardless of the translation of the preposition, the entire phrase may qualify either or both "repent" or "baptize." So to repent for the forgiveness of sins is in keeping with the message of Peter (cf. F. F. Bruce, *The Acts of the Apostles* [Chicago: Inter-Varsity Christian Fellowship, 1952], 98. A comparison of the use of the Greek preposition in the phrase here and in Mt. 12:41 would lead one to translate the phrase "in response to the forgiveness of sins." Either this or "in reference to" would be the best translation: meaning that one repented and was baptized in response to or in reference to the forgiveness of sins. After a study of this and other references in the Book of Acts, S. I. Buse, "Baptism in the Acts of the Apostles," *Christian Baptism* ed.

A. Gilmore (Philadelphia: Judson, 1959), 116, concludes: *"baptism . . . can hardly be described as either universal or necessary for salvation."*

7. Bruce, *Acts of the Apostles*, 215. For a definitive discussion of "God-Fearer" cf. K. Lake, *The Beginnings of Christianity*, 5 vols., ed. F. J. Foakes-Jackson and K. Lake (London: Macmillan, 1933), 5:74-96.

8. Buse, "Baptism in the Acts," esp. 116, 128.

9. F. Stagg, *The Book of Acts* (Nashville: Broadman, 1955), 105. Acts 19:1-7 is not a parallel to the baptism of the Samaritans since it is a case of disciples of John the Baptist being converted to discipleship of Jesus.

10. Buse, "Baptism in the Acts," 118f. rejects this interpretation.

11. F. J. Foakes-Jackson, *The Acts of the Apostles* (London: Hodder and Stoughton, 1931), 76.

12. Bruce, *Acts of the Apostles*, 194.

13. Luke's interest is not to give a detailed account of the geographical spread of Christianity, but rather to show how the gospel spread in all directions from Jerusalem to "men of all classes and races." Stagg, *The Book of Acts*, 108f. For the authenticity and use of this story cf. É. Trocmé, *Le "Livre des Actes" et L'Histoire* (Paris: Presses Universitaires de France, 1957), 179-81.

14. See above, 52f.

15. See below, 63-65.

16. K. Aland, *Did the Church Baptist Infants?* transl. G. R. Beasley-Murray (Philadelphia: Westminster, 1963), 90f.

17. Ibid., 89.

18. Buse, "Baptism in the Acts," 124.

19. Nor does 1 Cor. 1:16 argue for infant baptism. Again it is a reference to believers in Stephanas' household.

20. H. Bietenhard, "ὄνομα," *TDNT* (1967), 5:243.

21. Ibid.

22. Ibid., 245.

23. G. A. Deissmann, *Bible Studies*, 2nd ed., transl. A. Grieve (Edinburgh: T. & T. Clark, 1903), 147.

24. Bietenhard, *TDNT*, 5:267.

25. Ibid., 268.

26. Ibid.

27. See above, 21-26.

28. J. W. Bowman, *Which Jesus?* (Philadelphia: Westminster, 1970), 136-58.

29. Oepke, *TDNT*, 1:539.

30. K. Rengstorf, "ἀποστέλλω, κτλ," *TDNT* (1964), 1:431.

31. Ibid., 430; cf. Mt. 28:16-20; Lk. 24:36-49; Acts 1:8.

32. D. P. Fuller, "The Resurrection of Jesus and Historical Method," *Journal of Bible and Religion* 34 (1966): 22.

33. Oepke, *TDNT*, 1:539.

34. For the background of this assertion cf. B. Gerhardson, *Memory and Manuscript* (Copenhagen: Ejnar Munksgaard, 1961), esp. 324-35. E. A. Judge, "The Early Christians as a Scholastic Community," *Journal of Religious History* 1 (1960/61): 4-15.

35. It has not been the method of this work to burden the reader with detailed critical data; however, a word regarding Mt. 28:18-20 is in order.

The preceding discussion is based on the critical conclusion that the essence of the commission was delivered by Christ to his apostles in a post-resurrectional setting. Jesus commanded his disciples to make disciples, baptize, and teach. He intended that they take his message beyond the confines of Judaism. These assertions are based on the continuity that these commands have with the intent of Jesus' earthly mission. They are consistent with the teaching and preaching of his recorded ministry. Furthermore, it becomes quite difficult to explain the zealous evangelistic activity and baptismal practice of the earliest Christians if the command of Jesus were in fact only a formulation of the early church.

The trinitarian formula presents the most serious difficulty since none of the references in the Book of Acts requires a baptism in the name of the Father, Son, and Holy Spirit—only in the name of Jesus. This may be an occasion where the teachers of the church, during the period between Jesus' death and the composition of the Gospel of Matthew, rounded out the command of Jesus with a formula they had come to use in their prayers and rituals. If such a judgement should be made, it would in no way deny or alter the original intention of Jesus. The assumption followed in this text is that Jesus did commission his disciples to make disciples, baptize, and teach in his name. For further study on this point consult the references in notes 23-36 and also G. R. Beasley-Murray, *Baptism in the New Testament* (London: Macmillan, 1963), 77-92.

An excellent analysis of the problems involved in Matthew 28:19 is given by P. W. Evans, "The Baptismal Commission of Matthew XXVIII. 19," *The Baptist Quarterly*, 15 (1953-4): 19-28.

For the idea that Mt. 28:18-20 is not a post-resurrection command of Jesus but yet important because it is the continuing revelation to the church cf. F. W. Beare, "Sayings of the Risen Jesus in the Gospel Tradition: An Inquiry into Their Origin and Source," *Christian History and Interpretation*, ed. W. R. Farmer et al. (Cambridge: University Press, 1967), 161-81.

5 | *The Decision·*
Who Is Jesus?

In the drama of baptism one aspect is always present: the centrality of Jesus Christ. Because of him, for him, and in him baptism is a drama of the acceptance of Jesus of Nazareth as the bringer of salvation. Perhaps no writer stresses this idea as much as the author of the Gospel of John and the First Epistle of John:[1]

> But these are written that you may believe that Jesus is the Christ, the Son of God, and that believing you may have life in his name. (Jn. 20:31)

> Who is it that overcomes the world but he who believes that Jesus is the Son of God? (1 Jn. 5:5)

In other references it will be noted that John understands baptism as a drama testifying to this affirmation.

Jesus' True Identity

John is concerned to provoke his readers to a faith in Jesus as the Son of God. His entire Gospel was written to impress this belief on the minds of his readers, for the writer is faced with the scandal of apostolic Christianity: that the Christ could have been Jesus, an historical figure, or that "concrete human and visible flesh" could be of any significance for true religion.[2] The evangelist's purpose is to bring his readers to a faith which will be able to overcome such a scandal and accept the positive statement that "Jesus is the Christ, the Son of God." The writer has in no way

71

lessened the scandal, but has in some respects heightened it by emphasizing the humanity of Jesus. In no other Gospel is this element so prominent. *Jesus is a man.* This is a dogma in the Fourth Gospel.[3] It is Jesus who approaches John the Baptist (1:29) and who is followed by two disciples (1:37), and this man Jesus is known to those who follow him. He is a man of Nazareth, the son of Joseph (1:45), a man whose parentage is known, for the Jews question: "Is not this Jesus, the son of Joseph, whose father and mother we know?" (6:42). Indeed his family was known. His father has already been mentioned, and his mother appears in the Gospel. Whatever may be the significance of Jesus' reply to his mother at Cana (2:4), one thing is certain: the earthly mother of Jesus was recognized. Not only does she appear and is recognized at Cana but also at the foot of the cross where the reality of her presence can hardly be interpreted away on symbolic grounds. Such information as the parentage and earthly origin of Jesus was so well known it would have been futile to deny it. Even Jesus' brothers are known (7:3, 10); and they, like Jesus, are recognized as Galileans. That Jesus was a man of Nazareth is unhesitatingly affirmed in the Gospel. Not only did his first followers recognize that he was from Nazareth but so did his enemies, for the chiefs of the people seek to dissuade Nicodemus from following Jesus on the grounds that his origin is known (7:52). Furthermore, it is "Jesus of Nazareth" whom the guards seek to arrest and take to trial (18:5, 7), and it is "Jesus of Nazareth" whom Pilate gave over to be crucified (19:19).

This Jesus whose parentage and origin were known was a real person: that is he was beheld as a human being, possessing a corporeal body with its varied feelings and emotions. As a real physical being Jesus thirsted (4:6f.; 19:28); he expressed his emotions[4] at the tomb of Lazarus and also when he mentioned his betrayer (13:21; cf. 11:33). This man Jesus responded to the crucifixion as a human being. He expired (19:30); when his body was pierced, it responded as a human body (19:34); and his corpse was cared for after the normal manner (19:38-42).

It can hardly be denied that the evangelist has as vividly as possible portrayed the reality of the humanity of Jesus. Even his favorite title is "Jesus," which seems to add emphasis to the humanity of Jesus, for John has used this title more than any other of the NT writers.[5] It is the Jesus of history for whom the author is concerned, and he is anxious that the readers be made aware of the fact of his earthly, fleshly reality.

But the reality of the humanity of Jesus is not the only subject of concern for the evangelist. The predicate of his affirmation is just as important: *Jesus is "the Christ, the Son of God,"* and the two go together. In his ministry, Jesus' ability to perform signs, as well as the intended significance of them, emphasizes his role as Son. In the reality of his humanity, the Messiah-Son is able to act in such a way to reveal his true nature to those who care to understand. At Cana it is said: "This, the first of his signs, *Jesus* did" (2:11; cf. 4:54). When Jesus healed the man by the sheep gate, the man went away and told "that it was *Jesus* who had healed him" (5:15). Again, when the blind man is healed at the pool of Siloam, he goes away and confesses that "the *man* called *Jesus*" restored his sight (9:11).

Now Jesus is able to perform these wondrous deeds and thus reveal the glory of God only because of the unique relationship between himself and God. This relationship is described in terms of the father-son concept. Throughout the Gospel this concept is kept before the reader. The theme for this relationship is set by the evangelist in the third chapter: "The Father loves the Son, and has given all things into his hands" (3:35); and nowhere is the concept in the mind of Jesus more clearly treated than in chapter 5. Already before chapter 5 Jesus has been presented as greater than John the Baptist, as Lamb of God, as Son of God, as Messiah, as Son of Man, and Savior of the world; and following chapter 5 the great "I am" sayings occur. In what way are these claims of Jesus harmonized with his relationship to God? The discourse in chapter 5 makes this clear. "Jesus is what he is only in humble obedience to and complete dependence upon the Father."[6]

A fuller explanation is given because Jesus has claimed God as his Father and because there is a misunderstanding of that claim. "The Son can do nothing of his own accord, but only what he sees the Father doing" (5:19). In his miraculous deeds expressing the glory of God, Jesus has been submitting in obedience to a subordinate role in respect to the Father. Already in chapter 4 this understanding of the relation of the Father to the Son is set forth; it is to do the will of the Father that Jesus has come (4:34; cf. 6:38); and later in the Gospel it is the Father, who is greater than Jesus, who performs the works (14:10, 28). The claim of sonship on the part of Jesus is a submission to the authoriy of the Father (5:30)— a submission which expresses the utter dependence of the Son on the Father.

Just as clearly as Jesus claimed dependency upon the Father, so he also claimed a personal intimacy. Throughout the discourse in chapter 5, especially verses 19-30, the theme of the "unity of action between Father and Son" is repeated.[7] The claim of Jesus that he is executing a special mission for God mirrors this intimacy,[8] and Jesus claims to be involved in a life-giving (5:21; 6:40) and judging mission (5:22). This intimacy is complete, for there are no restrictions (3:35; 5:20); and it is abiding, for Jesus is never left alone (8:29). This intimacy is further emphasized by the fact that Jesus knows the Father (8:55)—a knowing which is possible because Jesus' origin is from the Father (8:42; cf. 3:13, 17, 31). So Jesus can claim that he is sent from God, not as a mere prophet or divine agent, but as one who bears in himself the power and glory of God.

This expression of Jesus' total dependency and utter intimacy with God is a reflection of his filial consciousness which has been understood in the father-son concept. This concept goes beyond the idea of dependency and intimacy, for this concept is capable of expressing the fact that someone shares the quality of another or something. The use of such a figure to express this concept is "due to the more vivid imagination of the oriental, who looked upon any very intimate relationship—whether of connection, origin or dependence—as a relationship of sonship"; so a "son of peace," "son of light," or a "son of the devil" is one who has in himself the qualities and nature of peace, etc.[9] When this relationship of father-son is used of Jesus and God it means not only that Jesus was dependent upon and intimate with the Father but also that he partook of the nature, character, and disposition of God. So intimate is this sharing and unity between the Father and Son that Jesus could say, "I and the Father are one" (10:30), or "He who has seen me has seen the Father" (14:9).[10]

Throughout the Gospel the evangelist has recognized the filial consciousness of Jesus as the inmost truth about himself and the clue to his outward activities;[11] yet the author has also retained the fleshly, concrete, earthly nature of Jesus. This is the heart of his dogma concerning Jesus. What is apparent in the entire Gospel has been given formal expression in the prologue, especially in v. 14: "And the word became flesh."

Jesus' actions revealed the glory and presence of the Father; and, if the Father and Son were so intimate that the Son reflected his very nature, character, and disposition, what better word could be used to summarize this expression of the Father than *word*. This term expresses more than what is meant by the

English term *word*; *it means the creative thought of God, the expression of his inner mind, the manifestation of his being.*[12] "The *logos* is God Himself as revealed"; it is "that of God which is knowable."[13] This understanding of the term is made clearer upon the examination of its use when the *word* of Jesus is spoken in the body of the Gospel. There it is evident that the meaning is not the usual sense of *word*, but rather the term *word* indicates the essential mind of Jesus. Jesus said, "If any one keeps my word, he will never see death" (8:51f.; cf. 14:23f.). Here it is quite obvious that the audible hearing is not intended, but rather that the hearers be in accord with the mind of Jesus.[14] As Jesus' words reveal himself, so *word* reveals the mind of God; and this is exactly what Jesus claimed—to reveal God to humanity. Because of this the evangelist can consider Jesus the subject of the statement: "The word became flesh" (1:14), for the author is able to write this and the entire prologue because of the Gospel, not the Gospel because of the prologue.[15]

This, then, is the scandal which the evangelist sets forth as his dogma. The expression of the mind of God found manifestation in the fleshly, concrete reality of a man—Jesus. In pinpointing the dogma the evangelist has used, on the one hand, the term *word* as an expression of the thought and will of God; and, on the other hand, he has used the term *flesh* to indicate the reality of the humanity of Jesus—humanity in its most humble, mortal, and temporary aspect. The writer is not here thinking of the union of two natures in one person as in Greek thought, but rather he speaks of the advent of the eternal will of God in the concrete reality of Jesus. For the author the divine has become human, the eternal has entered history, the plan of the ages has been made known. Yet he does not seek to understand the "how" and "why" of "the word became flesh"; he simply is summarizing what he has set forth in the body of the Gospel in an effort to state dramatically the dogma for which he is vitally concerned.[16] This is the distinctive mark of the evangelist—his faith in the reality of the incarnation.[17]

The evangelist has at every turn been concerned for the reality of the humanity of Jesus; this is a vital element in his dogma. However, this element has no significance unless the unique relationship between Jesus and God as set forth by the claims of Jesus himself are accepted. The author has delicately set forth the subject and predicate of his dogma through faith in spite of the scandalous obstacle. In the First Epistle the scandal is frequently stated in terse form, and the necessity of accepting it is just as demanding (1 Jn. 2:22; 4:3f.; 5:5). *To show the possibility of faith in this dogma the author has portrayed several characters as overcoming the scandal of the "word became flesh."*

It must be remembered that the evangelist's purpose is that his readers might believe that "Jesus is the Christ, the Son of God" (20:31). This is the affirmation which John the Baptist proclaims about Jesus (1:34), and Nathanael affirms that Jesus is "the Son of God" (1:49). In the light of the revelation which came to John the Baptist, his confession may be taken in the same sense as the author's general use of the term "Son" which is to express the father-son relationship as understood above. In the case of Nathanael it is possible that he sees in Jesus only a messianic figure with limited reign, but further understanding is implied. When Martha meets Jesus at the tomb of Lazarus, Jesus asks her if she believes that he is the resurrection. To this Martha replies that she believes that Jesus is "the Christ, the Son of God, he who is coming into the world" (11:27). Here Martha not only makes a confessional statement about his person but affirms that in him is true life. The achievement of this understanding of Jesus is exactly what the evangelist is seeking to accomplish in his work, according to his own purpose (20:31).[18] The evangelist has shown his readers that it is possible to overcome the scandal and see in the concrete reality of Jesus the presence, power, and mind of God. While all of the characters represented may have given expression to their confession in phrases with varying nuances of meaning, they all have recognized in Jesus one who is uniquely related to God.

The evangelist has presented Jesus as the one from God who brings salvation. The scandal of his earthly origin and human affiliations have not been eased. The claims of unique intimacy with God have blatantly been made. There is no hesitation to speak of Jesus' origin as being from the Father. The tension of the scandal is pointedly articulated in the statement: "The word became flesh." For the evangelist it all must be accepted; Jesus must be proclaimed Son. The only overcoming of the scandal is belief, and this is possible, for some have overcome.

The True Identity Recognized

In the Gospel of John the first person who recognizes Jesus as the bringer of God's salvation does so in the context of the rite of baptism. John the Baptist confesses that his baptismal activity is for the purpose of making the true Messiah known (1:31).

Although the Gospel of John does not give a detailed account of the baptismal activities of the Baptist, enough is said for the reader to know that the author was well aware of the setting of Jesus' baptism by John. That John did practice the rite is implicit in the question of the Pharisees: "Why are you baptizing?" (1:25)—and in the evangelist's geographical notices of the locality of John's baptismal activity (1:28; 3:26). It is part of the author's purpose to handle the John the Baptist material in such a way as to emphasize an aspect of the Baptist's baptism other than his mere practicing of it.

Unlike the Synoptic writers, the fourth evangelist neglects giving any explicit suggestion as to the meaning of John's baptism. He does not mention it either explicitly or implicitly as a baptism of repentance or as a time of confessing sins. The lack of such predication of John's baptism is to be expected in light of the fact that the fourth evangelist does not record John's eschatological preaching. Furthermore, the author does not use the baptism of Jesus to provide an understanding for the meaning of John's water baptism; however, the writer certainly knew of it,[19] for the record of John's testimony of the descent of the dove presupposes the baptismal scene. It seems almost an impossibility that an early Christian writer would not have known about Jesus' Jordan River baptism, and the fourth evangelist leaves ample room for it. His purpose in presenting the materials of the John the Bapist-Jesus encounter did not call for the use of the description of the event of the baptism; he simply assumes it. His purpose was first of all to reveal the hiddenness of the Messiah.

The author's apparent reluctance to deal in any way with the usual interpretation of John's baptism or of Jesus' acceptance of it is for a purpose. This purpose may be understood by the fact that for the author, John the Baptist's essential characteristic is not an eschatological preacher nor a practitioner of a water rite but that he gives a testimony to the author's essential dogma— "Jesus is the Son of God." This means that John, his testimony, and his activities must be understood along this line, for the author in the passages involving John directs everything toward his role as a witness.[20]

It is at the point of the Baptist's role of making known the hidden Messiah that the only hint of the author's understanding of John's baptism is found. The Baptist did not know who Jesus was, but in order that he (Jesus) might be made known he (John) came baptizing in water (1:31). It is not enough that John came; the peculiar attendant circumstance is significant, for John's

baptism was "the most conspicuous feature of his ministry."[21]
This is emphasized in that, contrary to the Synoptics who introduce John as simply appearing and preaching a baptism (Mk.
1:4), the fourth evangelist is aware that John was sent by God for
the purpose "to baptize with water" (1:33).

It cannot be overstated then that in the Fourth Gospel the
significance of John the Baptist's baptism has been emphasized
beyond the Synoptics in that it was an integral element of John's
divine commission and that it was an accompanying factor in the
revealing of the identity of Jesus. In other words John the
Baptist's vital message was: "I have been sent from God to baptize
with water; my baptism will reveal the unknown Messiah."

John's baptism is thus an attendant circumstance of the revelation of the revealer to Israel, and through this John carries out his
function. While the fourth evangelist records John as denying
that he is "the prophet" (1:21), he certainly recognizes John as
being in the prophetic tradition when he records the quotation of
Isaiah on the lips of John. Considering John as a prophet, the
fourth evangelist would have little difficulty in associating his
message or commission with his water rite and finding John's
purpose and testimony embodied in the rite. For the author the
importance of John's water baptism was focused at one point or
idea. The central purpose of John's rite was to reveal—to make
known the bringer of salvation.

The author's understanding of John's rite is taken only from
the point at which John came in contact with Jesus. The use of
the rite before or after this event has no relevance to the author.
John's rite embodied his purpose and commission and had
significance for the Christian tradition only at that time when it
revealed Jesus. Thus, for the fourth evangelist, John the Baptist's
water baptism was a factor in making known the hidden identity
of Jesus—revealing the Messiah to Israel. John's rite of baptism
in some way identified Jesus as the one uniquely related to God
and bringing salvation to man. It must be emphatically noted
that in John's Gospel the first historical episode relating to Jesus
is in a situation where his true identity is affirmed by one who also
confesses that his baptism is for the very purpose of making
known the Messiah. Baptism and the recognition of Jesus' true
identity are brought together.

*The writer John has called attention to the importance of
Jesus' identity in another context where there is a strong allusion
to baptism.*

> Who is it that overcomes the world but he who believes that
> Jesus is the Son of God? This is he who came by water and
> blood, Jesus Christ, not with the water only but with the water
> and the blood. And the Spirit is the witness, because the Spirit
> is the truth. There are three witnesses, the Spirit, the water,
> and the blood; and these three agree. (1 John 5:5-8)

Here John is stressing that the one who desires to overcome the
world through salvation must recognize Jesus as the Son of God.
Now John does not leave his readers without some evidence that
Jesus is the Son. He offers for their consideration three witnesses:
the Spirit, the water, and the blood.

First of all John emphasizes the importance of Jesus by desig-
nating him "he who came." This title of respect and honor
identifies Jesus as someone distinctive. In a unique way he came
"by water and blood." John uses "he who came" as a title of glory
and reverence suggesting that he is the one sent by God. He is a
divine envoy come into the world.[22] The author thereby stresses
that at a specific time and place in history Jesus, the Son of God,
appeared and was identified. To refer to Jesus as "he who came"
is another way of expressing "the word became flesh."

The once and for all coming of the Son of God in the historical
person of Jesus is further underscored by the "attendant circumstances" at his coming: he came "by water."[23] The coming of
Jesus is associated with a circumstance involving water. At a
specific time Jesus came; and the time, way, and event of his
coming is definitely identified by the words "by water." The event
of Jesus' coming designated thus can hardly be other than his
Jordan River baptism.[24] The author is recalling the Gospel of
John's account of how Jesus' Sonship was first manifest at his
Jordan River baptism. He is saying to his readers: "Remember
that when Jesus came to his water baptism by John the most
important thing was the revelation of his true identity. It is a part
of the historical material of the Gospel that Jesus' coming to his
water baptism was the occasion on which he was made known.
He came through water." In other words this was the event at
which Jesus' real identity was made known, the event at which
the incarnation was declared.

John is trying to turn his reader's attention to the way in which
the water of baptism was present at Jesus' coming in the past so
that they could relate the meaning of that past event to the
continuing practice of baptism at a later time. He has done this by
saying that Jesus *came* by water and that water continues to be a

witness.[25] The water of baptism is a symbol that recalls to the Christian the ultimate revelation made known in Christ, thus it can continue to witness to that past historical event. The baptismal water in the crucial event in the life of Jesus finds its continuation in the water of Christian baptism.

In John's Gospel account of Jesus' encounter with John the Baptist, and in 1 Jn. 5:5-8, the same theological idea is set forth, namely, that the water of baptism was connected with the true identity of Jesus. The water of baptism testifies "that Jesus is the Son of God."

The Drama of Recognition

Baptism by its very nature is an individual matter. It is the individual's response to the challenge to submit to the rite whatever its meaning. This is true of baptism as proclaimed by Peter (Acts 2:38). In the primitive church only faith and penitence on the part of the individual were required before baptism.[26] As the *kerygma* was proclaimed, the appeal to accept Jesus as Lord was made; and the convert who was willing to affirm, "I believe Jesus is Lord," further responded in baptism. Responding in baptism was for the individual convert a testimony of his acceptance of the message which he had heard, which message made known the real identity of Jesus.

Matthew very closely associates the proclamation of the gospel message and baptism by recording a post-resurrectional command of Jesus; in making this association, Matthew emphasizes the practice of the rite (Mt. 28:19). John gives significance to the rite of baptism by recording that Jesus himself baptized (Jn. 3:22). Although this is a rather definite notice bearing a geographical reference, the text later explains that it was not Jesus who baptized but only his disciples (4:2). It is hardly possible to dismiss the first notice as an invention by the author simply because no other Gospel writer has recorded it.[27] It is just possible that the writer here has access to an accurate primitive tradition. This may well be a trustworthy notice.[28] It is probably best to accept the later notice that it was not Jesus but his disciples who baptized as an explanation by an editor who was aware only of a tradition which said that Jesus did not baptize. Of all the possible places in John's Gospel, this parenthesis in chapter four, verse two, is the one most likely to be a later editorial addition.[29] On the other hand, the two passages together may have been introduced by the author to mean that, while Jesus did not baptize, he had authorized Christian baptism.[30] Whatever the disposition of the texts in question, the fourth evangelist has definitely recorded that Jesus and/or his disciples practiced water baptism, and it seems best to conclude that for the author *Jesus himself practiced the rite.*

That the event of Jesus' baptismal activity is somewhat significant is suggested by the fact that it introduces a new episode in the Gospel, and it is only after Jesus' whereabouts and activity are made known that the activity of John the Baptist is stated (3:23); he, too, is baptizing. Very little is said about this parallel baptismal activity of Jesus and the Baptist. It is emphasized that John's rite was in water. It is further noted that both baptizers drew people to themselves (3:23, 26) and the act of baptism seems to be emphatically related to the coming of the people before these two. Yet there is scarcely a hint as to the significance of that baptism.

True to the Johannine style, the author utilizes this historical setting as an occasion for a larger discourse. The occasion of the dispute between John's disciples and the Jews is passed over hurriedly and is only a small link in a stepped up chain reaction to provide John the Baptist with an opportunity to give a testimony to Jesus—his "final, most comprehensive, and enthusiastic testimony about Jesus. . . ."[31] In this testimony (3:27-30) the Baptist reaffirms that he is not the Christ but merely the one sent before him (3:28; cf. 1:19f., 23), for he is as a bridegroom's friend who makes ready the necessary arrangements. Now that the bridegroom is present and has taken his proper place there is no need for the friend; he has fulfilled his task. *In this, that Christ—the revealer from God—is recognized, John the Baptist consummates his life's work; and so he rejoices as one who has accomplished his mission* (3:29).

Either in his own words or in the words of John the Baptist, the author continues the testimony to the true identity of Jesus; and in a sense the final paragraph (3:31-36) of chapter three recapitulates the ideas of the entire chapter. This Jesus, who confronted Nicodemus, who was found baptizing in Judea, is the one who "comes from above"—he is of heavenly origin (3:31). As the revealer from heaven he gives testimony to the things he has seen and heard (3:32). This means that he "utters the words of God" and can be none other than the Son unto whom all things are given (3:34f.). The one who recognizes this role of Jesus as the true revealer of God believes unto eternal life (3:36). The force of this paragraph, as well as the entire chapter, is that Jesus is the complete revealer. He reveals himself as the bearer of eternal life to those willing to recognize his true identity.

John's testimony and the following commentary were set forth by the author at the occasion of an event in the ministry of Jesus. This is especially true in the early chapters of the Gospel as well as the later chapters. Such a use of events, however, does not mean that the event itself is not important, for the event and the characters involved may well add meaning to the following discourse.[32] The events cannot be overlooked. This is especially true in the case of Jesus' and John's baptismal activities—it has meaning.

John's Gospel, as noted above, presents the Baptist as one who bears witness; and his witness is embodied in his water baptism, for his baptism is an integral part of his commission and proclamation. So when the author records the Baptist's baptizing at Aenon, the reader must assume that here John's baptism bears the same significance that it did in chapter one. At Aenon John's baptism, like his testimony, would be an attestation to the true identity of Jesus—he is the revealer. At this point the evangelist sets side by side the baptismal activity of Jesus and John, and seemingly he provides no explicit definition of either. The least that can be said is that they were similar, for neither the question raised by the Jews nor the report to the Baptist by his disciples is concerned with any difference. The author implies that the two baptizers practiced similar rites.

The coming and submission of individuals to this water rite presuppose a proclamation and an acceptance of it. The Baptist's proclamation here can be none other than his previous witness: "I am come, baptizing, to reveal the revealer." The author intends that the reader assume that some such proclamation preceded Jesus' baptismal activity. In other words, Jesus' proclamation would be that he himself is the revealer from God and that baptism is the embodiment of that proclamation.

This understanding of the meaning and significance of Jesus' baptismal activity is substantiated by the immediate context. *In the context of the Nicodemus episode Jesus is presenting himself as the revealer sent from God.* This is the theme of the entire discourse and succeeding comment. This was the theme which led to Nicodemus' misunderstanding of Jesus' identity. Nicodemus' misunderstanding is set in contrast to the Baptist's testimony in the last part of the chapter. In the recapitulation paragraph

(3:31-36) it is noted that some have accepted and some have rejected Jesus' identity, and certainly the reader is to understand that some accepted and submitted to Jesus' baptism. Then Jesus' baptism would be a witness to his identity as it embodied his proclamation; and the individual, as he submitted to Jesus' baptism, would be dramatizing his testimony to Jesus' true identity—namely, Jesus is the revealer.

This is the author's understanding of the baptismal activity of Jesus: it is a testimony to Jesus' true identity. For the fourth evangelist the baptism of Jesus is closely akin to the baptism of John; both testify to the fact that Jesus is the revealer sent from God. The recording of Jesus' and John's parallel baptismal activity is probably the author's effort to connect the church's baptism with that practiced by John as well as to establish it in a vital relation to Jesus' ministry. This he has done by associating the baptismal activity of Jesus and John both in proximity of practice and similarity of meaning.

With the foregoing in mind, Jesus' discussion with Nicodemus about being born of water makes sense: "Unless one is born of water . . ." (3:5). Because of the author's previous emphasis on the Baptist's water baptism in chapter one and his recording of the baptismal activity of Jesus and John later in this chapter, it seems reasonable to assume that "water" in Jn. 3:5 is an allusion to baptism.[33] It has been argued, however, that such a reference is in no way related to baptism but rather to the idea of celestial waters from which come life-giving, living water, the divine gift.[34] While such an idea cannot be ruled out altogether, for the author is certainly capable of using words with overtones, the reader is certainly reminded of baptism.

To discern a reference to baptism in the term "water" is consistent with the previous understanding of baptism as well as with the immediate context where "water" is associated with birth, rebirth, or birth from above. The idea of rebirth in Jn. 3:5 has a common background with "in the new world" of Mt. 19:28.[35] Matthew uses the concept in the usual manner of referring to participation in the future messianic era, while John has used it to stress his understanding that eternal life is already a present possession. He is declaring that a new beginning comes only from God as he has made it known through Jesus, the revealer of eternal life. The recognition of Jesus in this role is a new beginning comparable to birth. The idea that the author sought to convey in these words of Jesus was that a new life is available to the one who recognizes him as the revealer of that life. Such a recognition of the true identity of Jesus and the gift of eternal life comes only through faith and the work of the Spirit, but it is bound with and totally dependent upon the true identity of Jesus. The water of baptism embodies and declares that identity. It is the open recognition of one's acceptance.

To be born of the water of baptism is to be born of the message embodied in baptism or, to express it another way, to be born of the witness of the water of baptism. It is the acceptance of the witness of baptism—that Jesus is the bringer of salvation—which gives birth to salvation in the individual; this is the new beginning. In this sense the water of baptism is a witness to the individual of the true identity of Jesus, for it was in the water of baptism that he was revealed; and, furthermore, in the water of baptism the individual testifies to his acceptance of the true identity of Jesus—for this is the proclamation embodied in baptism.

John's understanding of baptism is that the water rite is a witness. In the mission of the Baptist it testified to the identity of Jesus. Jesus and/or his disciples practiced the water rite which again is understood by the evangelist to testify to the true identity of Jesus. Jesus' practice of baptism gave continuity both to the rite of water baptism and its meaning. This continuity in meaning is maintained in that baptism is understood as a witness to the true identity of Jesus; and its proper significance for the individual is understood not only from John's baptism, or from Jesus' baptismal activity, but also from the figure of birth "of water." This water baptism the church accepts and proclaims as a dramatic testimony to the true identity of Jesus. By accepting baptism the individual not only dramatizes his recognition of Jesus as the giver of salvation, but he further participates with the entire church in giving testimony to the identity of Jesus.

The Drama at the Cross

The early church's proclamation was simply "Jesus is Lord." This is seen in Peter's Pentecost sermon as well as the basic *kerygma* of the church. The individual's acceptance of the water of baptism was a confession of this proclamation. Beyond the simple participation of the individual in the rite, baptism was a proclamation within itself; it was one of the church's activities which proclaimed its message, and its message was centered in the death and resurrection of Jesus.

In the record of the crucifixion of Jesus according to John's Gospel, an unusual incident is immediately noticed as additional information beyond the Synoptics. The soldiers come and pierce the side of Jesus while he is still hanging on the cross (19:34). The resulting phenomenon draws the attention of the reader, for *from the pierced side of the crucified Jesus flows blood and water.* It is quite obvious from the following verse (19:35) that the evangelist intends to record an ocular testimony; what he describes was actually seen. The eyewitness observed a phenomenon which he recognized as blood and water flowing from the side of Jesus. While a modern physician may have described his observation of the phenomenon in different terms, it is physiologically possible for an event to have occurred which could have been described as blood and water flowing from a wound. At this point it was the author's intention to describe an actual happening while Jesus was on the cross.

The insistence of the author that this event is attested by an eyewitness suggests that the evangelist considers the happening important, not simply as an incident, but because of its meaning, for it is a part of the evangelist's literary style to record an historical event to express a theological truth.

It is altogether possible that when he wrote this passage with the record of the flow of blood the evangelist had in mind an early false doctrine which denied Jesus' true humanity. So, for those who would say that Jesus was a mere phantom when he died, the evangelist has recorded that blood "which is common to mortal humanity" flowed from the pierced side.[36] This would contradict any idea that could later be formulated to report Jesus' saying that no real blood flowed from his body (Acts of John 97, 101). The recording of this event refutes the same false teachings that the First Epistle argues against in several places (1 Jn. 4:2f.). The lance thrust proves that in death the body of Jesus of Nazareth was a human corpse.[37] For the evangelist this event bears the same message which he has given in the prologue: "The word became flesh." To record the flowing of blood alone would have emphasized this understanding; however, the writer has further recorded the flowing of water from the pierced side.

This additional element of *water* may simply confirm the humanity of Jesus as did the flow of blood, for there is some suggestion that ancient Jewish physiology understood that man existed from one part blood and one part water. A rabbinic account points out that the wrong proportions would cause illness, and in 4 Maccabees 9:20 one of the slain brothers emits blood and bloodwater.

On the other hand, the Greeks understood that the gods, who were immortal, were bloodless; however, they were not anemic, but hydremic; for their blood was watery. The Greek writers used the term *ichōr* for this bloodwater of the gods. So when Diomedes pierces the hand of Aphrodite with his spear, the blood that ran from the wound was not red but *ichōr*. A passage from Plutarch emphasizes that only blood and not bloodwater issues from the wound of man. When Alexander the Great had been hit by an arrow and was suffering, he said: "This, my friends, that flows here, is blood, and not *Ichor*, such as flows from the veins of the blessed gods." Such a background as this may suggest that the inclusion of water along with blood in the record of this event emphasizes the divinity of Jesus.[38]

It is possible then to conclude that the appearance of blood from the wound would attest to Jesus' true humanity and the water would suggest his true divinity. It is doubtful, however, that the evangelist thought in such rigid categories. It seems best to understand the event of the spear thrust and the fluids flowing from the wound as a testimony to the reality of death of Jesus, for the evangelist is seeking "to provide evidence that Jesus was a real man, and that he really died."[39] This understanding of the event is further supported by the following comment that "He who saw it has bourne witness . . . that you also may believe." The testimony of this eyewitness is to lead the readers to belief not only in the specific event but also in the gospel itself, *for the event, by attesting the reality of the humanity and death of Jesus, affirms the basic dogma of the evangelist that Jesus, who is claimed to be the Son of God, did come in the flesh.* This is the burden of the author as he writes. So when the author states that a given event is for the purpose of producing faith, it cannot be passed over as simply meaning acceptance of the veracity of the witness; it must further be accepted as a testimony to produce faith in the full meaning of the term for the evangelist. For him faith is the recognition that Jesus of Nazareth is the Son of God sent from God as Savior of the world.

Beyond this basic understanding of this event as a testimony to the reality of the death of Jesus and thus to his true identity, there is another aspect of the meaning. The first readers of the Gospel could hardly miss an allusion to the Eucharist and baptism in the mention of blood and water. Had the writer desired to emphasize only the reality of the death of Jesus the spear thrust and the effusion of blood would have sufficed. The addition of water brings into clear focus the possibility that here is a specific allusion to the early Christian rites. A reference to the rites is far more likely than finding these elements symbolic of the cleansing and regenerating efficacy of the life and death of Jesus, or symbolic of the reconciliation brought about by a new covenant established in the church—the new Eve, which came forth from the side of Christ; the fourth evangelist seems little concerned for any idea of sacramental cleansing or regeneration. The author's use of the OT at this point (19:37) does not help in understanding the elements, since the possible texts quoted (Ex. 12:46; Num. 9:12; Ps. 34:20) do not mention a flow of blood to be connected with the sacrificial system, nor do they seem to have a specific relation to Johannine theology.[40]

On the basis of the promise of the gift of the Spirit and its relation to Jesus' death (7:38f.), the effusion of water may be taken as the gift of the Spirit to the disciples; however, the explanatory remark about Jesus' offer of living water does not say that the Spirit will be given at the crucifixion, but that the Spirit was not yet given "because Jesus was not yet glorified" (7:39). The gift is specifically related to Jesus' glorification, but the language of the explanatory note cannot be pressed to mean that the gift must come simultaneous with the crucifixion; and, since the evangelist records a giving of the Spirit after Jesus' death, it seems better to find the fulfillment of Jesus' promise there (20:22). There can be little doubt that the record of the insufflation is intended to fulfill the previous promises of the Spirit.

In the sense that living water has been associated with life-giving (4:10, 14; 7:38; 3:5), it is altogether fitting to find in the water flowing from Jesus' side a reference to the efficacy of the cross, for the evangelist understands Jesus' glorification at his death as the source of life. Jesus, not the church or sacraments, is the one from whom comes life. He is the salvation bringer, the one sent from God as the Savior of the world. What the eyewitness sees in this event is a testimony to the work and nature of Jesus. He witnesses that indeed this is the Son of God, the bringer of salvation, the giver of life; and his testimony is recorded that the readers might also believe.

Therefore, *it is altogether fitting to find in this episode a definite reference to water baptism.* The author has already made possible the association of baptism with Jesus' death when he recorded John the Baptist's exclamation—"Behold, the Lamb of God, who takes away the sin of the world" (1:29)—at Jesus' Jordan River baptism. The evangelist has made clear that there is a relationship between Jesus' baptism and the mission he is to fulfill in pointing to his death at the time of his baptism, for baptism finds its final and significant meaning as it is related to the cross.[41]

The difficulty does not so much lie with the problem of accepting water at this point as an allusion to baptism as with the significance of such an allusion. This in no way suggests the efficacy of baptism as a sacrament—as that which gives or transmits life; nor does it suggest baptism as a cleansing or purifying rite. The allusion is to baptism as a testimony—a testimony to the person of Jesus. This is in keeping with the above understanding of the entire event; both the ocular testimony and the record of it by the evangelist point to one idea: this is in reality Jesus, the one sent from God, who has died on the cross. The testimony is to the true identity of Jesus. This is the testimony which baptism bears. The evangelist provides previous indications that he understands baptism in this respect, and to accept baptism as a testimony at this point is consistent with the evangelist's mind. Just as the physiological phenomenon of the flow of blood and water testify to the reality of the humanity and death of Jesus, so also the allusion of water to the rite of baptism testifies to the same—the reality of the incarnation. Baptism then for John is neither a magical rite nor an efficacious sacrament, but a testimony to the real identity of Jesus, the Son of God.

Thus the church had a constant testimony to the true identify of Jesus in the rite of baptism. As the rite was performed, it recalled, to those who observed, Jesus' glorifications, the reality of his death, his true nature and work. This was the continuing witness of "water" in the church.

§

At first glance it does not seem that the Gospel of John is concerned for the rite of baptism; however, on further examination it appears that he gives enough hint here and there to formulate his understanding of the meaning of the rite.

The evangelist so emphasizes John the Baptist's baptism as a testimony to the true identity of Jesus that it becomes the theme for the author's further understanding of Christian baptism. The baptismal activities of both Jesus and John become occasions for further testimony to the true identity of Jesus. It is here that the meaning of baptism for the individual is a testimony. As the individual participates in the rite he testifies to his belief in the true identity of Jesus. It becomes the individual's drama of testimony. Further, the objective witness of baptism as it is practiced in the church recalls the reality of Jesus' crucifixion and his true nature. Baptism bears testimony to the true identity of Jesus on Jesus himself, for the individual, and within the church.

For the author of John, baptism is a witness to his basic message that Jesus is the Son of God. This means that baptism testifies that Jesus, who came in the flesh, is the Savior of the world. This removes baptism from the realm of a magical, sacramental rite with any efficacious meaning and makes of it a proclamation of the evangelist's key theme—"the word became flesh." This makes baptism a pointer to the one who mediates life. It is indeed a drama both of the individual's decision to accept the salvation brought by Jesus and of the church's continual affirmation that he is her Lord!

5

NOTES

1. In this chapter the name John, fourth evangelist, et al., will be used synonymously to designate the author of the Gospel of John and the First Epistle of John without entering into the critical attempts to determine the exact identity of the author.

2. E. C. Hoskyns, *The Fourth Gospel*, ed. F. N. Davey (London: Faber & Faber Ltd., 1947), 52.

3. F. C. Burkitt, *The Gospel History and Its Transmission* (Edinburgh: T. & T. Clark, 1911), 233.

4. This is true regardless of the interpretation of ἐμβριμάομαι in Jn. 11:33. C. K. Barrett, *The Gospel According to St. John* (London: S.P.C.K., 1955), 332, is certain that the term implies anger; Jesus is angry because the Jews and sisters of Lazarus are forcing a miracle upon him. Hoskyns, ibid., 403f., interprets the term as describing Jesus' passionate grief; cf. *BAG* (1957), 254.

5. V. Taylor, *The Names of Jesus* (London: Macmillan, 1954), 6f. The title "Jesus" in 1 John also emphasizes his historical humanity. Cf. 1 Jn. 2:22; 4:3; 5:1; and B. F. Westcott, *The Epistles of St. John*, 2nd ed. (Cambridge/London: Macmillan, 1886), 137.

6. Barrett, *St. John*, 214.

7. Ibid.

8. C. J. Wright, *Jesus: The Revelation of God*, Bk. 3 of *The Mission and Message of Jesus*, eds. H. D. A. Major, et al. (New York: E. P. Dutton, 1938), 681.

9. Deissmann, *Bible Studies*, 161ff.; Wright, *Jesus*, 681.

10. This same meaning for the father-son concept is present in 1 John: The unique intimacy is recognized (1 Jn. 2:23), and the idea of the life-giving mission of Jesus is present (1 Jn. 1:2; 4:14). The use of the title "Son of God" in the First Epistle, like the Gospel, expresses the unique filial relationship between Jesus and the Father. Cf. A. M. Hunter, *Introducing the New Testament* (London: SCM, 1957), 149; Taylor, *Names*, 69f.

11. Wright, *Jesus*, 680.

12. Ibid., 678f.

13. C. H. Dodd, *The Interpretation of the Fourth Gospel* (Cambridge: University Press, 1955), 277, 280.

14. Wright, *Jesus*, 679.

15. For a complete analysis of the concept "word" in Hebrew and Greek thought, esp. Philonic thought, and its cosmological meaning, cf. Dodd, *Interpretation*, 263-85. For an emphasis of the biblical and Judaistic background of the term, cf. Dom Jaques Dupont, *Essais sur la Christologie de Saint Jean* (Bruges: Edition d l'Abbye de Saint-Andre, 1951), 13-58.

16. A summary statement expressing the same general theme is found in 1 Jn. 1:1-4; cf. W. F. Howard, *Christianity According to St. John* (London: Duckworth, 1943), 54; Dupont, *Essais*, 43.

17. "On peut donc amintenir que la marque distinctive due 4ᵉ Evangile, c'est sa foi en la *realite de l'Incarnation* . . . L'Incarnation chrétienne se presente comme une *Historie:* l'histoire de Jesus." Henri Clavier, "Le Problem du rite et du mythe dans le quatrieme evangile," *Revue d'Histoire et de Philosophie Religieuses* 31 (1951): 281.

18. Cf. the confession of the man who had been healed from blindness, Jn. 9:37f.

19. Barrett, *St. John*, 148; Wright, *Jesus*, 718; M. Goguel, *Au Seuil de l'Evangile Jean-Baptiste* (Paris: Payot, 1928), 161.

20. O. Cullmann, *Early Christian Worship*, transl. A. S. Todd, J. B. Torrance (Chicago: Henry Regnery Co., 1953), 61f.

21. J. H. Bernard, *A Critical and Exegetical Commentary on the Gospel According to St. John*, ed. A. H. McNeile (Edinburgh: T. & T. Clark, 1928), 1:48.

22. M. Barth, *Die Taufe—Ein Sakrament?* (Zollikon/Zurich: Evangelischer Verlag AG, 1951), 396. A. E. Brooke, *A Critical and Exegetical Commentary on the Johannine Epistles* (Edinburgh: T. & T. Clark, 1948), 134f.; cf. Mt. 11:3; Lk. 7:19 where John the Baptist questions whether Jesus is the coming one. J. Bonsirven, *Épîtres de Saint Jean* (Nouvelle ed.; Paris: Beauchesne et Ses Fils, 1954), 229; cf. Jn. 1:11; 5:43; 13:3; 16:27f., 30; 17:8.

23. The change from δία to ἐν in v. 6 is purely stylistic; cf. Barth, *Die Taufe*, 399. For a contrary view see Bonsirven, *Épîtres*, 230, n. 1: "δία se refererait a la manifestation historique; en au sacrement qui demeure."

24. Barth, *Die Taufe*, 399; Flemington, *Doctrine of Baptism*, 88f.; E. Schweizer, "Da johanneische Zeugnis vom Herrenmahl," *Evangelische Theologie* 8 (1953): 346.

25. The writer has very carefully chosen the verb tenses that would express his thought. "He who came" is an aorist participle emphasizing an event in the past while "witnesses" is a present participle emphasizing

the present, continuing activity. Cf. Flemington, *Doctrine of Baptism*, 90; Westcott, *Epistles*, 184.

26. Recall ch. 4; cf. W. Robinson, "Historical Survey of the Church's Treatment of New Converts with Reference to Pre- and Post-Baptismal Instruction," *JTS* 42 (1941): 42.

27. Cf. R. Bultmann, *Das Evangelium des Johannes* (Göttingen: Vandenhoeck & Ruprecht, 1960), 122.

28. M. Goguel, *The Life of Jesus*, transl. O. Wyon (New York: Macmillan, 1933), 275: "We are forced to regard this source as an ancient document"; cf. Flemington, *Doctrine of Baptism*, 30f.

29. Bultmann, *Das Evangelium*, 127; Dodd, *Interpretation*, 311, n. 3; Wright, *Jesus*, 739.

30. Hoskyns, *Fourth Gospel*, 227.

31. E. L. Titus, *The Message of the Fourth Gospel* (New York: Abingdon, 1957), 100.

32. Nicodemus may represent the presentation of Jesus to the Jewish nation; the episode with the Samaritan woman is Jesus' offer of life beyond the Jewish nation.

33. Barrett, *St. John*, 174f.; Cullmann, *Early Christian Worship*, 75; W. F. Howard, "Introduction, the Gospel According to St. John," *The Interpreter's Bible*, eds. G. A. Buttrick, et al., (New York: Abingdon-Cokesbury, 1952), 8:445, and "Johannine Sayings of Jesus," *Expository Times* 46 (1934-35): 490f.

34. The idea presented here has been summarized as: "Water as Divine Efflux—Celestial Waters—waters from above—Life-giving, Living Water—The Divine Gift coming down from on high—waters of Eternal Life—Waters of Eternal Truth." H. Odeberg, *The Fourth Gospel* (Uppsala Och Stockholm: Almqvist & Wksells Boktryckeri-A-B., 1929), 67.

35. Dodd, *Interpretation*, 304; cf. 1 Enoch 25:1-6; 50:1; 2 Baruch 51:1-10; 1 Cor. 15:51f.

36. Wright, *Jesus*, 931.

37. For a discussion of John's use of the term "blood," see the author's article, "The Johannine Eucharist," *JBL* 82 (1963): 293-300.

38. For further discussion of the background of ancient Jewish physiology, cf. H. J. Cadbury, "The Ancient Physiological Notions Underlying John I.13 and Hebrews X.11," *Expositor*, 9th series 2 (1924) 430-39; P. Haupt, "Philological Studies, No. 5: Blood and Water," *American Journal of Philology* 45 (1924) 53-55; Schweizer, "Das johanneische Zeugnis," 341-63.

39. Barrett, *St. John*, 462.

40. Cf. *La Sainte Bible* (Paris: Les Edition du Cerf, 1956) 1427, n.j. for the last idea. For typical interpretations by the Fathers, cf. Bernard, *Gospel According to St. John*, 2:648, and Hoskyns, *Fourth Gospel*, 534f. For commentators who take the two elements as indicating regeneration and purification, see Hoskyns, ibid., 533 and Wright, *Jesus*, 931.

41. N. Clark, *An Approach to the Theology of the Sacraments* (Chicago: A. R. Allenson, 1956), 18; cf. Cullmann, *Early Christian Worship*, 64f. The Synoptics also make a connection between baptism and the cross: Mk. 10:38; Mt. 20:22; cf. Clark, ibid., 16f.; Oepke, *TDNT*, 1:540 for the idea that baptism receives its validity from the reconciling transaction of God in Christ, precisely from the atoning death of Christ.

6 | The Drama of Participation

More biographical information is available about the Apostle Paul than any of the other NT writers. Thanks to the author of Acts a sketch of his adult life is preserved. Perhaps this is one of the reasons many students of the NT are attracted to his literary work and accept his writings as the height of early Christian theology. Whatever Paul's rank in a list of apostolic theologians, there is no question that he made a major contribution to first-century Christianity's understanding of the event of Jesus Christ. One can readily appreciate Paul's theological emphasis by reading Romans, Galatians, or Ephesians; and the contemporary student is not without countless volumes analyzing his thought.[1]

Unfortunately, for those who would desire elaborate answers on specific points, Paul does not render the service of telling his reader how to practice baptism and exactly what it must mean each time it is practiced; yet he has not failed to make several references to it and perhaps implicit allusions as well.[2] This is understandable since his letters are written to churches, recently established, in which he either practiced the rite himself or approved others who performed it. This would involve some explanation of the meaning of baptism. That is to say when Paul wrote his letters, the recipients had already received baptism and had been taught its meaning; thus the briefest reference to it would recall the entire theological content to Paul's readers. The modern reader is simply denied the privilege of reading Paul's sermon or lecture on baptism. Because of this lack of explicit discussion, Paul's understanding of baptism must be viewed against the panorama of his gospel message in general and the context of specific reference in particular.

Paul's Gospel

There is a certain urgency in Paul's efforts to proclaim the gospel, because he is convinced that humanity, both individually and collectively, suffers a self-imposed *predicament of alienation* from God. This aspect of Paul's gospel is especially apparent in Romans 1:18-3:20. From his Hebrew heritage he accepts as a presupposition of his argument that God the Creator has manifested himself through his created handiwork. This implied a certain dependency of humanity upon God, but enticed by its own ability it sought to determine its own destiny rather than acknowledge any dependency upon God (Rom. 1:18-32). God permitted human beings the privilege of freedom of choice along with the responsibility for those decisions. So God did not prevent human actions that result in suffering. The world, blinded by its passion for absolute independence, created a society filled with injustice, suffering, and death. In this alienated state there was little hope. Humanity, by refusing to accept its role as a creature, had thrust itself into a state of moral ineptitude totally estranged from God.

This estrangement was so complete that Paul could at times picture the individual-out-of-relation-to-God as one who was controlled by the evil forces at work in the universe. "The sons of disobedience" were as opposite to God-related-man as the one who is dead is different from the one who is alive. He was enslaved to superstitions and deities which were really not gods at all. Humanity, by denying its dependency upon God and by absolutizing secondary things, became so far removed from God that it could not, by its own efforts, return (Gal. 4:8-11; Eph. 2:1-8).

Or to say it another way, mankind absolutized its own decision-making abilities and rejected any need for a higher absolute, namely God. Paul, being a Jew, singled out his people for specific consideration (Rom. 2:1-3:8). Their problem: they had absolutized the Law and had taken pride in their relation to it. This had the effect of insulating them from God; so they too were alienated, estranged.

For Paul such an analysis explained the gross immorality of humankind, the gross idolatry that existed in the Graeco-Roman world, and the suffering human beings imposed upon one another. Furthermore, it gave insight to the problem of the Jewish concern for Law and their lack of sensitivity to Paul's gospel. All of this does not necessarily argue for a distorted pessimism in the mind of Paul; but rather, it is an effort to understand mankind's plight in the universe. If an individual could only come to terms with God, his entire existence would surely be different. Furthermore, a statement of condition or need is necessary as a prelude to a presentation of the corrective. Paul must set the stage of humanity's predicament in order to dramatically present God's corrective—Jesus Christ!

In a context describing mankind enslaved to the superstitions of the universe, Paul poignantly proclaims that "when the time had fully come, God sent forth his Son" (Gal. 4:4) as *the final answer to humanity's predicament.* Christ is the means by which the alienation will be removed, people can be freed from their commitment to anything less than God, and they can begin to order their existence out of dependency upon God. For Paul, Christ gave mankind a new understanding of itself and its universe because he put it in touch with God. This idea begins to be worked out in Col. 1:15–20.

> He is the image of the invisible God, the first-born of all creation; for in him all things were created, in heaven and on earth, visible and invisible, whether thrones or dominions or principalities or authorities—all things were created through him and for him. He is before all things, and in him all things hold together. He is the head of the body, the church; he is the beginning, the first-born from the dead, that in everything he might be pre-eminent. For in him all the fullness of God was pleased to dwell, and through him to reconcile to himself all things, whether on earth or in heaven, making peace by the blood of his cross.
>
> (Col. 1:15-20)

Here our early theologian stresses that Christ is that which explains the created order. Christ unlocks the secrets of the universe. In him meaning for all of creation and humanity's place in it is discovered. In the first place Christ is the ideal human being—the model from which humankind was created. By stating that he is the "image" of God, Paul is alluding to Gen. 1:26f. where God determines to make man in his own image. This ensures that the reader will not miss the place of Christ in the creative process. Adam, and consequently all mankind, was created after the pattern of Christ.[3] By adding the title "first-born," Paul has added a further concept from his Hebrew background. The first-born son, cattle, or any living thing, belonged to God. It must either be sacrificed to God or redeemed by sacrifice as a sign that God still retained some claim on all that followed. At the same time the first-born was the promise that more like it was to follow—the first of other like occurrences.[4] By applying this title to Christ the intention is to heighten the declaration that he is the model, the pattern, by which humanity can understand what being human really involves. What does it mean to be a human being in a created order? This was (and is) the ultimate question. For Paul the answer was simple—Christ!

In the second place Christ is so bound up with the totality of creation that Paul grasps for concepts that will in some way approximate his thought. "In him," 'through him," "for him," the creation was ordered. The conditions calling for the created order, the instrumentality in creation, the purpose or goal of creation, all center in Christ. Whatever question, reflection, or surmise about the universe and humanity's place in it finds its satisfaction in him. For Paul, Christ is the "primordially meaningful word"[5] upon which *all* understanding rests. "In him all things hold together." He is the ultimate, the absolute, that which brings coherence to human knowledge and inquiry. In him mankind begins to comprehend the ultimate: "For in him all the fullness of God was pleased to dwell."

In the third place, Christ, who is the foundational understanding to all existence, is the one who reconciles an alienated world to God. Christ's unique position qualifies him to remove humanity from its predicament of estrangement. In Paul's thought humanity is out of contact with God by its choosing to absolutize its self-understanding and by declaring its radical independence. The experience of mankind was convincing evidence that this did not work. The corrective was obvious to Paul: the correct understanding of human existence in the created order is found in the one who stands at the very core, depth, foundation of the universe, namely Christ. To discover, or accept meaning in Christ is tantamount to accepting dependency on God; for God, who is responsible for the centrality of Christ, dwells in Christ.

This idea is restated in Eph. 1:9-10:

> For he has made known to us in all wisdom and insight the
> mystery of his will, according to his purpose which he set forth

> in Christ as a plan for the fullness of time, to unite all things in
> him, things in heaven and things on earth.

The intention of God is to reconcile, "unite" mankind to himself, and not just mankind, but the totality of the universe. There is a design for the created order, and that design is Christ. Here is the position, the vantage point, from which all human understanding must take its departure if it is to comprehend and cooperate with the design of the universe. Mankind must recognize its dependency upon God by accepting God's agent of reconciliation. This is summarized in the saying: "In Christ God was reconciling the world to himself" (2 Cor. 5:19).

Now in Paul's Gospel God's response to the human predicament is vividly and concretely portrayed in *the death, burial, and resurrection of Jesus*. This event is the *sine qua non* of Paul's theology. To this point and from this point flow all considerations of God's dealings with humanity. In Corinth, Paul "decided to know nothing among you except Jesus Christ and him crucified" (1 Cor. 2:2); and he reminded the Galatians that before their "eyes Jesus Christ was publicly portrayed as crucified" (Gal. 3:1). Paul's interpretation of this event as God's action toward humanity became the basis for his position on the human predicament and the role of Christ. He insists that what happened at the cross is the very thing that reconciles mankind to God: "making peace by the blood of his cross" (Col. 1:20), "And you . . . he has now reconciled . . . by his death" (Col. 1:21f.).

However the world evaluates Christ crucified, the event can only be understood as the wisdom and power of God (1 Cor. 1:24). Here Paul deliberately chooses the two symbols representing ultimate understanding to his readers. To know power, to know wisdom were from a human standpoint the height of attainment— they gave meaning and satisfaction to human existence. For Paul, Christ crucified is God's answer to mankind's search for such significance and satisfaction. Yet the cross must be interpreted by the resurrection, and the Lord can be none other than the crucified Jesus.[6] That is to say the death, resurrection, exaltation of Jesus comprise a totality that cannot be disengaged; for, just as certain as he emphasizes the cross (death), he maintains the absolute necessity of the resurrection: "If Christ has not been raised, then our preaching is in vain and your faith is in vain" (1 Cor. 15:14).

The cross and resurrection of Christ are given data in Pauline theology. His effort is not to move by reflection to a particular intellectual stance for which these concepts are symbols, for he had met the executed, resurrected Christ near Damascus. Out of this encounter Paul accepted the Christ-event as God's action to mankind. It was God's wisdom, God's power. The task of the theological reflection of Paul begins with the given data and presents it in the best thought patterns available. He accomplishes this in continuity with the Hebrew heritage of the gospel and in response to the Graeco-Roman culture.

In one paragraph (Rom. 3:21-26), Paul interprets the meaning of the cross through a variety of descriptive terms. Jesus is the one who brings "righteousness." This is a judicial term which reminds the reader that Christ is the one who makes mankind right before God. Or Paul can use the word "redemption" which has its background in the freeing of a slave (1 Cor. 6:20; 7:23, Gal. 3:13; 4:5). Christ is the one who frees man from the bondage that keeps him away from God. Christ is also sent as an "expiation." The overtone here is sacrificial with probably an allusion to the mercy seat in the holy of holies in the temple. It was to this holy place that the high priest came once a year to make atonement for the sins of the entire congregation. At the mercy seat God met the representative of mankind (the high priest) and forgave its sins. Paul is making an effort to verbalize what took place in Christ's death and resurrection: God has now set forth Christ as the locale where he meets humanity and is reconciled with it.[7]

In other places Paul refers to Christ's death as a Passover sacrifice (1 Cor. 5:7), as a representative sacrifice (2 Cor. 5:14), as a ransom (Gal. 3:13), and other symbols. Each effort is to understand the meaning of Christ's death. How has it brought salvation, how can the human mind understand and the tongue speak of it?

Additional help in understanding the cross-resurrection event is forthcoming when the resurrection aspect is considered. (A discussion at this point is valuable since some of the baptismal references are in contexts that speak of a resurrection.) Paul's understanding of the resurrection of Christ is apparent only in the context of Jewish eschatology. As already pointed out,[8] this doctrine may be briefly outlined as follows: (1) There is an end to human history when the world of mankind will be transformed to conform to the will of God. This will be a utopian era or the kingdom of God. (2) This era will be inaugurated by the coming of the Messiah and presence of God's Spirit. (3) A confrontation between the righteous and unrighteous will take place, and God and/or the Messiah will intervene on behalf of the righteous. He will make them victorious. (4) All the dead will be resurrected, judged, and rewarded. The righteous will enter the kingdom forever.

Paul certainly has this general background in mind, as did the early Christians. From 2 Thessalonians 2 it is obvious that Paul is thinking in terms of point three, that period when good and evil will be in deadly combat. The "man of lawlessness" embodies evil (v. 3), which is the Jewish background of Paul's eschatological thought as further noted in his relating the return of Jesus with the resurrection of Christians who have died (1 Th. 4:13-18). Throughout Paul's writings there is a strong conviction that the believer will be resurrected at the coming of the new era (Phil. 3:20f.; Rom. 8:11; 1 Cor. 15:35, 51f.).

Now how does this help in understanding Jesus' resurrection from Joseph's tomb? It is evidence that God had already broken into human affairs in the very way that Jewish theology anticipated. The resurrection, a circumstance of the beginning of the new era, a sign that the new age was present, has already begun. Exhibit A of the certainty of the new era is on display: Jesus is resurrected. Paul's emphasis, with one exception in 1 Th. 4:14, is that God raised Jesus (cf. Rom. 4:24f.; Gal. 1:1).[9] God therefore has given a sign of the certainty of the new era. God is already breaking into human history; the age of renewal has dawned, and a resurrection has taken place. This offers hope and stimulates confidence in the future participation in the resurrection era. Paul confesses on one occasion that he desires to know the "power of his resurrection . . . that if possible I may attain the resurrection from the dead" (Phil. 3:11). His hope is that he will participate in the future resurrection. If he does so it will be because the power of Jesus' past resurrection convinced him that Christ was able to "change our lowly body to be like his glorious body" (Phil. 3:21).

The future resurrection of the believers was guaranteed by Christ's resurrection. He was the "first fruit." Paul specifically draws a line from Christ's resurrection to the assured future resurrection in 1 Corinthians 15. His whole theology rests on this connection. Faith that God has intervened in the affairs of humanity, hope that the righteousness of God will ultimately triumph over evil, certainty that the believer will be resurrected into the new era, all hinge on the reality of Christ's resurrection (vv. 12-19). Verses 23f. of this chapter show that Paul's eschatological framework stems from his Hebrew background. The kingdom, the new era, will emerge for the resurrected righteous.

Paul interpreted the death of Christ in the thought pattern which he knew from his own Hebrew theology and that of the primitive church. The idea of a future resurrection was not new. The hope of the righteous participating, though frequently dulled, was part of Paul's heritage. But the new dimension that brought renewed hope was a sample—a genuine resurrection—that convinced men and women of faith that God was not only going to bring about a resurrection in the future, he had done it now! There would be a future renewal of all things in the kingdom, and evidence for that renewal was already present in the resurrection of Christ! Here was power, here was wisdom. This was indeed verification that Christ was God's answer to humanity's predicament.

Jointly, Christ's death and resurrection meant that God had acted in the affairs of humanity in such a way as to heal the predicament, remove the alienation, and reconcile mankind to himself giving it hope for the future. The death and resurrection were the concretizing of God's offer. As has already been suggested above, this creates a right relationship with God; mankind is set free; it has a place (in Christ) where it can meet God. Now Paul makes an effort to describe further *the individual who has accepted God's answer to his predicament.*

This individual is a person of faith. The concept of faith is not treated academically by Paul but rather explained by giving an example. After describing God's gift of Christ in Rom. 3:21-26, Paul turns to elaborate the fact that faith is the human response to God's offer in Christ. "For we hold that man is justified [becomes righteous before God] by faith . . ." (Rom. 3:28). In order to vividly portray what he means, Paul turns to the story of Abraham. Abraham's response to God's offered promise, as recorded in Gen. 15:6, is acclaimed: "Abraham believed [had faith in] God, and it was reckoned to him as righteousness" (Rom. 4:3). That is Abraham was made right with God on the basis of his faith-response to God's offer. Paul urges that faith is not a matter of accumulated knowledge or academic research, rather faith rests solely on one's willingness to accept the offer of God as authentic and to believe that God is able to produce what he promises. To illustrate this very vividly, Paul reminds his readers that Abraham, being about one hundred years old, was as good as dead; Sarah was obviously beyond the age of bearing children. Yet he was "fully convinced that God was able to do what he had promised" (Rom. 4:21). Now this has application to Christians: "It [righteousness] will be reckoned to us who believe in him that raised from the dead Jesus our Lord" (Rom. 4:24). Christian faith then, for Paul, is simply accepting as authentic the ultimate word from God spoken in Jesus. God promises reconciliation, a remedy for humanity's predicament; individuals accept the promise and God's ability to perform it. That's faith!

The response of faith to God's offer in Christ is a revolutionary experience for the individual. A person orders his or her life according to certain goals, ambitions, and values. Out of these a pattern of existence is styled that will best accomplish these goals. The human being has developed an orientation to life. A continual striving to find satisfactory meaning for life takes place. Then God's word in Christ is encountered. It is accepted as the ultimate meaning for existence, for Christ is the "image," the "first-born." The individual discovers a new orientation, a new meaning, new answers. The change is so stupendous that it strikes at the very nature of human existence. Paul's Damascus road encounter with Christ so profoundly impacted his very existence that his reflection upon it is apparent in his writings.

> I have been crucified with Christ; it is no longer I who live, but Christ who lives in me; and the life I now live in the flesh I live by faith in the Son of God, who loved me and gave himself for me.
>
> (Gal. 2:20)

In this climactic confession concluding the first two chapters of Galatians, Paul articulates that his present life takes its design from his faith in the Son of God. In Christ he has found God's affirmation of all of his divine promises (2 Cor. 1:20). This called for such a radical reorientation of his existence that Paul could say there was something new and different in him—namely Christ. The old inner self has died and been replaced by Christ. He is indeed a new man.

To the ancient Hebrew mind the word "creation" was charged with more uniqueness than in contemporary thought, for "creation" carried with it the idea of something distinct, never before existing. When a creation takes place, it can hardly be compared with any previous phenomenon. So Paul further describes the inner change of the man of faith by saying "If anyone is in Christ, he is a new creation; the old has passed away, behold the new has come" (2 Cor. 5:17). The source of this new creation is God, and the medium through which it comes to humanity is Christ (2 Cor.

5:18f.). Something new and startling has happened to the one made righteous through faith in Christ. Paul can at times contrast the new and different state of existence of the "before" and "after" individual of faith by such pairs of terms as "life" and "death" (Eph. 2:4-10) and "slavery" and "freedom" (Gal. 4:1-31).

In chapter 8 of Romans and chapter 5 of Galatians, Paul describes this new creation, with its new inner self, as a person who "walks," i.e., conducts his or her life, by the Spirit. This Spirit comes from God (1 Cor. 2:12) and becomes the motivating force in the life of the new person. It gives direction to the life of the individual of faith in such a way that his or her actions are consistent with the new inner being. In both of the passages noted here, the person oriented and motivated by the Spirit contrasts the person oriented and motivated without faith. The latter conducts life according to the "flesh."

Such an analysis of Paul's thought about the changed condition of the person of faith may well be understood from the background of the modern use of the term "self." Human beings seek to understand themselves in terms of their relation to the total world order—their environment. They strive to have an image of themselves that not only includes this but that also embodies some understanding of their destiny in the universe. Out of this understanding a person fashions behavior patterns and orders conduct. He or she develops a lifestyle, or it may be said that he or she achieves selfhood—self-identity. There is a wholeness to the person. At least to a minimal degree, this individual comprehends the meaning and intent of existence. The word "self" is a referent to the capacity of a human being to integrate personal existence in a meaningful way.

This is apparently what Paul is trying to get at when he describes the change in the person of faith. He has now come upon a new understanding of life at its depth—the point from which it takes its meaning, the direction toward which it flows, and the course it will follow. This, of course, is God's offer to humanity in Christ. To accept this is to be "with Christ," "in Christ"—it is to discover a *new self.*

Now, the individual of faith did not come to that new existence in isolation, but rather in community. Through the community of faith the word of God was proclaimed in such a way as to produce faith. Paul's missionary enterprise began in the context of the community of faith in Antioch, and in each area that Paul traveled he left behind the small communities of faith—men and women who had responded to this proclamation. Whenever an individual came into his or her new existence, that one immediately became a part of a *new community.*

This new community became known by the word "church." Paul always thinks of Christians in relationship to one another. It never concerns him to advise the person of faith how to live alone. All the letters that Paul writes are addressed either to churches or "Christians" in the plural. Even Philemon is addressed to more than one person; and, although addressed to specific individuals, the content of the Pastorals deals with churches. There was simply something about becoming a new person before God that thrust the individual into community with others of like experience. That is to say the church was immediately constituted by those who had been reconciled to God.

Just as the individuals learned a new dependency on God through Christ, the community recognized its intimate relation to Christ. Paul refers to the church as the "body of Christ" in order to illustrate this close association. In speaking to the Corinthians, he reminds them that they "are the body of Christ and individually members of it" (1 Cor. 12:27). This was said not only to show their dependency on Christ but to remind them of their close relationship to one another. In Eph. 1:22f. the figurative language is fully applied, and Christ is designated the head, and the church is the body. Paul suggests the meaning he intends this symbol to convey by noting that Christ is "the head over all things for the church." In a position of authority and dignity he acts on behalf of his new community which in turn fully expresses his will. The new community is so intimately related to Christ that it depends upon him for its very existence and can only be an expression of his mind. The use of marital language in Eph. 5:21ff. further highlights this intimate association. There Christ, like a worthy husband, loves the church to the extent of giving his life for it. While the church, like a faithful bride, is subject to Christ in everything.

Paul understands, then, that the reconciling act of God in Christ, not only makes a new creature of the person of faith, but it also creates a new community. As the person of faith owes his or her new existence to Christ, so also the church is totally dependent on Christ.

This new community has two functions to perform. First it is to further the development of the new person. A person develops in the community. The new person can further develop his or her understanding of personal destiny in Christ by interacting with fellow Christians. In Eph. 4:11-16 all the various functions within the church are to have one goal: "for building up the body of Christ." This inner development of the church must continue until "we all attain the unity of the faith and of the knowledge of the Son of God, to mature manhood, to the measure of the stature of the fulness of Christ." The new community is that place where men and women of faith develop, grow, mature, understand, and gain knowledge. Always the model or image toward which they strive is Christ.

Second, by its very existence the new community bears witness to the reconciling power of God's act in Christ. The church was called into existence by Christ, it exists as dependent upon him. Where it is present, those who observe it will know the reason for its being. It demonstrates by the relation of member to member that it embodies a force that can reconcile human beings to one another because of the reconciling power of God in Christ. This might be called the passive or indirect testimony of the church. But it is also entrusted with a direct or active testimony—proclamation. It heralds the good news of Christ's reconciling power. This proclamation is made so "that through the church the manifold wisdom of God might now be made known . . ." (Eph. 3:10). The new person functioning in a new community as evidence of God's reconciling power was an inevitable result of God's act in Christ.

This new understanding of self in relation to God and others that the individual of faith discovered demanded some concern for *a new ethic* for a new style of life. Paul shows no hesitation in delineating certain activities and attitudes that are unbecoming to the individual of faith. Lists of vices appear in Gal. 5:19-20; Col. 3:5-8; Eph. 4:17; 1 Cor. 5; 6:9; 2 Cor. 12:20, et al. On the other hand, he will list those positive attributes worthy of the new person. These are found in Gal. 5:22-23; Col. 3:12-15; Phil. 4:8. He even speaks on specific matters from time to time. Household codes are found in Col. 3:18-4:1 and Eph. 5:21-6:9, while advice on marriage appears in 1 Corinthians 7. These references make it quite obvious that Paul expected a high and noble ethic of his fellow Christians.

Paul's ethic is not legalistic. Here the distinction must be made between legalism and law or rules. Legalism connotes a devotion to law or rules for the sake of the rule, viewing the keeping of rules, laws, precepts as a means of salvation. Paul deals with this in Romans 7 and Galatians 3, concluding that the Christian is free from the law as a means of salvation, and at the same time he offers specific guides for the style of life consistent with the new creation in Christ.

Although Paul does not treat the area of moral conduct exhaustively, two paragraphs illustrate the general direction of this thinking. In 1 Corinthians 8 Paul deals with the problem of eating meat that has been consecrated to an idol. Paul does not give a "yes" or "no" answer. Rather, he delineates what might be called freedom to responsible action. "You are free to make your own decision, but you are responsible for your actions," seems to be the gist of the chapter. Being responsible obligates one to take a look at the secondary or contingent effects of his actions, first upon himself. Paul reminds his readers that the Christian is not as strong as some think, and sometimes actions may weaken one's own conscience (v. 7). Then the Christian is further responsible for the effect of an action on a fellow Christian (vv. 12f.), who is of inestimable worth since Christ died for him or her. This chapter in 1 Corinthians identifies what might be called the principle of responsible freedom. For Paul, Christians were free to act, to make their own decisions, so long as they recognized their responsibilities for the effects of their actions, first on themselves and then on their fellow believers (cf. Rom. 12:3-8).

Paul's ultimate ethical norm is set forth in Phil. 2:1-11. Here he is trying to inspire Christians to fitting conduct in relation to others. So he turns to the example of Christ and challenges his readers to think and act like Christ whose concern was obedience to God and the welfare of mankind. The final guide to Christian conduct is the example of Christ.

Now Paul's theology comes into focus. Humanity is in a miserable predicament, alienated from the one source that can bring meaning to life. God, aware of this predicament, sets forth Christ as the instrument which can reconcile humanity to himself, removing the estrangement and offering new meaning to life. The combined event of the cross and resurrection is the center of God's divine activity. It is the given. It means that a new dimension, the new era, has already broken in upon human existence and God has given evidence that he will fulfill his promise. By responding in faith the individual claims God's promise which creates a new existence—a new self. The creation of this new self is brought about by and further augments the new community, the church, which fulfills its role in God's plan. The new self, within this new community, will develop and mature as it works out a style of life after the example of Christ, the final norm for Christian conduct.

Here then is a theological analysis of Paul's thought out of which one may understand many more specific interests of the apostle. The immediate interest is baptism. When Paul refers to the matter of baptism it is usually in an oblique manner. He uses the word "baptize" in an illustrative way. Assuming the readers are already initiated into the meaning of the rite he alludes to it briefly to augment his point. Unfortunately his letters do not offer specific directions regarding baptism as they do the "Lord's Supper" as in 1 Cor. 11:23-26. Because of the limited material on the subject, it is all the more necessary to understand with some degree of thoroughness Paul's theological position as well as his flow of thought in each of the sections in which a reference to baptism appears.

Belonging to Christ

Paul's own baptism and his practice of it as attested by the Book of Acts were discussed previously.[10] It may be recalled that Paul's personal experience convincing him of the legitimacy of Jesus' messiahship culminated in baptism, an act that firmly associated him both with Christ and with those who also proclaimed him Lord. When one turns to Paul's epistles, it is discovered that this is the way he treats baptism. It is an act that declares the close, intimate relation between the believer and Christ.

This is the case in Galatians 3:27—"For as many of you as were baptized into Christ have put on Christ." Obviously the apostle is recalling to the minds of his readers their own baptismal experience and its meaning. His purpose here is not to elaborate the doctrine of baptism, but rather to use baptism and its meaning to help his readers grasp the point he is seeking to establish. After his confession that Christ now lives in him—a life that is based on his faith in the Son of God (2:20), Paul raises the either/or question to the Galatians: "How did you receive the Spirit which enlightens unto salvation? Either by works of the Law or by hearing and responding with faith?" (Gal. 3:1-5). Of course, the answer to the question is patent for Paul, but from this point of departure he wishes to strengthen his readers' conviction that they are truly sons and daughters of God because of their association with Jesus, an association based on faith (3:26).

To argue this point Paul returns to God's promise of salvation to Abraham as recorded in Genesis 12 and 15 (Gal. 3:6-9). Here he understands God's declaration to Abraham—"In thee shall all the nations be blessed"—as a proclamation of the gospel which one day would be extended to the Gentiles *by faith.* Since Abraham's response to this promise was faith, and since God accepted Abraham as righteous because of his faith, Paul concludes that those who have now responded in faith are blessed along with Abraham. Thus faith is more important than Law.

What about the Law? In vv. 10-14 Paul argues that the Law had become ultimate for some because of human misunderstanding. That is to say, some completely relied on the Law for their salvation. Instead of salvation such reliance brought a curse as the Scriptures themselves verify. It is Christ who frees humanity from the curse of its misunderstanding by bringing adequate understanding of God's salvation (v. 13). To be cursed is to be removed from the blessings and promises of God, to be outside his salvation. This is the result the Law brings to those who rely on it. For Paul, Christ in his death became the accursed. Men relying on the Law executed him. He was momentarily outside God's blessings. He experienced what was the person-dependent-upon-the-Law's just end. Through Christ's death (and resurrection) God demonstrated his will to extend the promise made to Abraham to the Gentiles. By faith they can receive the promise of the Spirit. In this way Christ has freed humankind from its misunderstanding of the Law. Again, faith is superior to Law, but in this paragraph Paul brings out the association of believers with Christ through faith. Believers are associated with Christ as he sets them free.

The apostle is not yet satisfied; he wishes to look at the matter again so he gives the example of a man's will which is considered inviolable (vv. 15-18). The will or promise made to Abraham was that in his "offspring" (singular, not plural) i.e., Christ, the nations would be blessed. This is the gospel. When Christ appeared he was indeed the heir of the promise. He was the one bringing blessings, promise, and salvation to everyone. No amount of legislation can cancel or alter the will made to Abraham. After all, the Law to Moses came "four hundred and thirty years" after the will was made. This cannot alter the inheritance that God promised to all. Here the Law is not as effective as the promise of an inheritance for God.

Some digression must be made by Paul to explain the usefulness of the Law (vv. 19-22). He does this by capitalizing on the imagery of inheritance introduced in v. 18. If there is an inheritance, there are heirs; but the heirs were not of age, yet immature; so the Law served as a custodian of the heirs until the appointed time when the offspring would come making the will or promise effective. This means that the Law was useful but not ultimate; it could not replace faith in the promised offspring who would bring the gospel of salvation.

Now that the promised one has come, faith is the response the potential heirs must have. Those who do respond are made righteous on the basis of their faith. They are like Abraham (v. 9). Exactly to what are the heirs responding in faith?—to *the offspring* to whom was given the promise of blessing everyone. The *offspring*, Christ, comes; he claims to offer salvation from God, and he is the heir of God's promise. Do men respond to this faith or continue to rely on the Law? Now those who respond to Christ in faith are associated with him in sonship (or daughtership, for that matter) to God (v. 26). A new status has been granted. This concept of sonship is further elaborated in Gal. 4:1-7, especially vv. 4f. Here Christ, *the offspring*, is identified as God's Son sent to activate the promise, free men and women from their misunderstanding of the Law, so that they might become sons and daughters of God. The Spirit (4:6) which the believer receives by faith (3:2) makes it possible for them to address God as Father (4:6), being no longer slaves (4:7).

By the time Paul comes to 4:7 he has adequately answered the opening question (3:2). He argued that at every point the Law is inferior to faith. *Faith is the only effective reaction human beings can have toward God.* The content of that faith is Christ Jesus who is the fulfillment of God's promise to all mankind, through Abraham. Those who respond in faith enjoy a unique relation to God; they are his sons and daughters. Sonship is achieved by faith—association with *The Son*, Christ Jesus. He associated with mankind in such a way as to demonstrate the utter futility of relying on the Law, for it destroys. He became a Son under the Law so human beings could associate with him, be redeemed from the Law and enjoy, through him, an intimate relationship with God.

Two concepts in this section (Gal. 3:1-4:7) cannot be over emphasized—redemption (3:13; 4:4f.) and sonship (3:26; 4:5ff.). These two terms show how Paul understands the Christian's intimate association to Christ Jesus. In both cases of the word "redeem," it is Christ who redeems. Recalling that the background of the word is the manumission of a slave, the aspect of the slave's thanks and devotion to his emancipator cannot be overlooked. A bond of fellowship one for the other will be created. In other places Paul can speak of Christians as belonging to Christ because they have been "bought with a price" (1 Cor. 6:19f.; 7:23).[11] On thinking of salvation under the concept of redemption there is the inherent aspect of belonging, to some degree, to the one who has redeemed.

In the Galatian context Paul defines this sense of belonging. Christ redeems so that individuals may be adopted sons and daughters of God (4:5), thus being identified with Christ who is *the* Son. They share with him the status of sonship. The redeemed become like Christ in their relation to God. He is the pattern to which all believers conform as he creates a new group of people. By being associated with Christ something new takes place; the believer is different; he or she enjoys not only a new fellowship with Christ but also with fellow believers. In Christ a corporate solidarity is created (Gal. 3:28).

According to the above analysis of Gal. 3:1–4:7, Paul stressed that God sent his Son, Christ Jesus, as the heir of the promise to Abraham. He, the Son, will bless all those who respond in faith—a kind of faith like Abraham's.[12] Those who respond to Christ are intimately associated with Christ, they enjoy a new relation to God, one of Sonship, like Christ.

In the light of this interpretation the baptismal text is understandable. With the word "faith" reverberating from v. 26, in the first part of v. 27 Paul reminds them that they "were baptized into Christ." There is no apparent difference in the phrase "into Christ" and "in the name of Christ."[13] It was suggested earlier that to "baptize into or unto" is best understood as "baptized in reference to or with a view toward" and that "to baptize in the name of" means to become a possession of or to belong to someone.[14] So Paul is simply recalling that those who have been baptized did so as a sign of their belonging to Christ.

The second part of the baptismal sentence posits that those participating in baptism "have put on Christ." Both the word "baptized" and "put on" in v. 27 grammatically refer to a past event, and the sentence certainly links the "putting on" with the "baptism." The word translated "put on" means literally "to dress" or "to clothe," thus one wears something. When used in the figurative sense, as it is here, it means that one exemplifies or is known by the characteristic, virtue, or trait he puts on. So in Col. 3:12, when Paul introduces a long paragraph of admonitions by saying "Put on . . . ," he wishes his readers to exemplify the qualities or virtues he lists. Be like this! This idea of putting on is extended to the entire personality in Eph. 4:24 where the Christian is admonished to "put on the new man, the one created similar to God." [15] There is something of a kinship between this concept and that in Col. 1:15 where Christ is the one who is the image of God—the one like or similar to God. So in this verse the Christian is being exhorted to become like Christ. Likewise Col. 3:10 calls for a putting on of the new in the likeness of its creator. Again, this is a reference to the new understanding of life which Christ brings. The idea of putting on Christ is not a novel phrase to the baptismal passage in Galatians. In fact, it is a normative idea in Paul's thought and is clearly articulated in the references where he insists that the believer has become a new creation. [16] What Paul wishes to stress is that those who were baptized became like Christ in that they embody the very characteristics and likeness of him. [17]

In this context Paul uses the symbol of "sonship" to identify the new relation that exists between God and the person of faith after the pattern of Christ's sonship. It would be fitting to suggest that when Paul says you have put on Christ he is thinking of Christ the Son. "You have put on a sonship like Christ's.

Now the crux of interpreting Gal. 3:27 lies in the question of whether or not Paul understands baptism as the medium or instrument that effects the likeness of Christ in the baptized. [18] Does baptism clothe one with Christ? There is no evidence in the OT that the Hebrews saw some mysterious, miraculous force in a ritual producing the intended result or change in the person participating in the ritual. To the contrary, the importance of the prior experience and disposition of the individual is stressed. This is true in the OT, in rabbinic literature, as well as the writings of Qumran. [19]

Of course Paul could think contrary to his heritage and pattern his ideas after the mystery cults, but the context of Galatians 3 argues against this also. For the major emphasis throughout the chapter is on faith—unrestricted and unqualified, without stimulation from a ritual. Faith is the only effective response to the promise of God, the declaration of the gospel. Faith and "hearing with faith" (3:5) are the theme of the entire chapter. These associate human beings with Christ and allow participation in a new relation to God. There is no suggestion in the context of chapter 3 that Paul thinks of baptism as a ritual affecting a change in the life of the individual. On the other hand, everything in chapter 3 stresses faith as the one condition for association with Christ.

What then is Paul's understanding of baptism from Gal. 3:27? The entire chapter is trying to restate convincingly the essential truth of the gospel he had preached to the Galatians. Faith, redemption, and sonship are his chief themes. The believer is described as one who hears, responds in faith to the redemption effected by Christ, and he or she now enjoys a new status with God because of an association with Christ's sonship. To recall this to the believer's mind in a vivid picture, Paul reminds them of their baptism. "Don't you remember what you were doing when you were baptized? You were portraying your association with Christ, you were declaring that you had become like him. Because you had heard and believed you vividly dramatized your decision to belong to him." The very fact that Paul could only briefly mention baptism attests that it was well understood by both his readers and himself. So he can use it to recall an event which both he and the Galatians understand as a summary of all that he is saying in this context. *They belong to Christ in a most intimate way. Baptism dramatizes this belonging.*

This understanding of baptism by Paul and his converts is obvious in 1 Cor. 1:10-17. Here there are some members of the Corinthian church who erroneously pride themselves on belonging to Paul, Apollos, Cephas, or Christ. Evidently some deflected the true meaning of baptism and found a secondary attachment to the administrant. Paul corrects this misappropriation of baptism, for he is anxious that they identify the one to whom they belong by remembering the one in whose name they were baptized. From this rhetorical question (v. 13) he and they understand that legitimate baptism is in the name of Christ.

Again in 1 Cor. 10:1-5 Paul illustrates his understanding of baptism as a rite that attests that the baptized belongs to the one named in the act. In recalling the story of the Exodus from Egypt, he comments that the Hebrews were "baptized into Moses in the cloud and in the sea" (v. 2). Now the Hebrew people were associated with Moses, they belonged to him.[20] He was their leader, his destiny was their destiny. Whatever his welfare, they would share it. Although Paul does not intend to equate that baptism with Christian baptism, the basic meaning is the same and helps in understanding Paul's idea about baptism. This paragraph also supports the idea that baptism does not effect an assured spiritual condition, for the very point Paul is making is contrary. He is trying to impress the Corinthians that although the believer might participate in significant religious rituals, even baptism, neither personal faithfulness nor ultimate salvation are thereby guaranteed (v. 5). Baptism, then, is an act of the individual who has responded in faith—an act dramatizing that by faith he belongs to Christ.

Association with His Death

If Paul can recall baptism to the minds of his readers in order to remind them of their close association with Christ, it is not surprising that he can bring together baptism and the death and resurrection of Jesus, especially since the latter figures so prominently in Paul's theology as the locale where the believer encounters the meaning of Christ. Rom. 6:3f. does this:

> Do you not know that all of us who have been baptized into Christ Jesus were baptized into his death? We were buried therefore with him by baptism into death, so that as Christ was raised from the dead by the glory of the Father, we too might walk in newness of life.

Again it is evident that Paul is recalling baptism to emphasize the point he is making, since the context does not elaborate the meaning of baptism but rather develops another idea. In these verses baptism already had a meaning for Paul's readers that was inherently related to the context. This would immediately augment his argument. The reference to baptism would relate his ideas to a concrete experience of his readers. Thus the meaning of baptism in this text is available only from an understanding of the flow of thought in the apostle's mind.

The Book of Romans is the most comprehensive and coherent statement of Paul's theology. He begins with a succinctly stated thesis:

> For I am not ashamed of the gospel: it is the power of God for salvation to every one who has faith, to the Jew first and also to the Greek. For in it the righteousness of God is revealed through faith for faith; as it is written, "He who through faith is righteous shall live."
>
> (Rom. 1:16-17)

By analyzing the state of mankind, both Gentile and Jew (1:18-3:8), Paul concludes that all are estranged from God (3:9-20). The opportunity to overcome this estrangement and be reconciled is offered to mankind by God through the gift of his Son. Humankind accepts the opportunity by responding in faith (3:21-31). What is the reconciled individual like? He or she is a person who has expressed faith (ch. 4). Here as in Galatians, Abraham's response to God's promise becomes the text from which Paul exemplifies the importance of faith. Abraham exemplifies what Paul understood faith to be.

The centrality of faith in this early part of the Book of Romans is significant. The effectiveness of the gospel in the believer is dependent upon faith. In the statement of the thesis (1:16-17) faith is one of the key words. The gospel brings salvation to those who have faith. Faith-righteousness makes alive. When Paul describes the plight of estranged humanity in chapters 2 and 3, the factor of faith is absent. There is none! Then when he returns to God's act in 3:21ff. faith is integral to everything. God's righteousness is made manifest "through faith in Jesus Christ" whose expiation is "to be received by faith," and God will make righteous "him who has faith in Jesus Christ."

In chapter 4, Abraham, the man of faith, is made righteous because of his faith even before the rite of circumcision which was only a sign of righteousness through faith. Faith for Abraham, as Paul understood it, was the tenacity to accept God's promise against all odds. Because of his faith Abraham was reckoned to be righteous. This reckoning was not only for Abraham but for Paul's readers so that they would understand that this right relation to God depended upon their faith in the reconciling death and resurrection of Jesus as the power and gospel of God. The place of faith as the determinative response of the individual to God's offer of salvation is foundational for understanding the subsequent-chapters in Romans.

Now the reconciled person is a person of faith whose hope in the future controls his present life (5:1-11). Because one has been declared righteous before God on account of faith, he has peace with God (v. 1) and hope (v. 2) of sharing in an even more intimate relation with God. This hope is augmented by God's love which was displayed in the death of Christ (v. 8). It is an individual's faith in the death (blood) of Christ as a reconciling event that makes him or her right with God; moreover, it is the certainty of Christ's resurrection (the dawn of a new era) that affords the hope of being spared the consequences of God's future judgement (vv. 9–10).

The time scheme in the background of Paul's thought here is Jewish eschatology which conceived of a final judgement, during which the messianic era would begin in victory and splendor. The person of faith can approach this end with serenity because God's love is already extended in the reconciling death of Christ. The resurrection of Christ assures the reconciled individual that he or she already shares, to some degree, the blessings of the new era. This, in turn, provides hope of full participation in God's final salvation. Such thinking on the part of the apostle reflects two significant eras in the history of humanity's relation to God. On the one hand is the era of Adam from which the believer is freed, and on the other hand is the era of Christ to which the believer is being saved.

When Paul notes in Rom. 5:12 that sin entered the world through one man, he is simply stating the contemporary rabbinic interpretation of Genesis 3.[21] As the Jewish theologians reflected upon Adam and his sin (fall), they tended to aggrandize his image before his sin and describe his disastrous estate after the Fall.[22] In this paragraph of Romans Paul does not enter into an expanded discussion of the origin and universality of sin.[23] Rather, he simply assumes that *Adam is a fitting symbol of the era of sin and alienation from God.* Adam introduced sin into human history, and thus death came. So Adam represents all mankind who likewise have sinned. Adam was the bringer of an era, and all living in that era with its life of sin and estrangement partake of the nature of Adam. He sums up and incorporates into himself all humanity in its estranged estate, standing in the need of reconciliation. There is a commonality among men. As they are descended from Adam, so they are all together sinful. Thus Adam becomes the image of man the sinner.

This image of Adam is precisely the backdrop to compare and contrast the new era introduced by Christ. In other texts (Col. 1:15; 1 Cor. 15:45–50) Paul underscores the heavenly origin of Christ, for the Fall had such far-reaching effects that nothing short of a heavenly Messiah could bring in a new era.[24] *Christ, the second Adam, has the power to incorporate into himself the new era and a new humanity.*[25] Even in this paragraph Paul cannot help but continue to emphasize the death of Jesus as he did in the previous one (vv. 6, 8, 9, 10). It is because of one man's act (v. 18) and one man's obedience (v. 19) that the new era is introduced.

Because of "Jesus Christ our Lord" (v. 21), the new period of grace will lead to eternal life. Christ is the bringer of a new era, a new relation to God, a new style and pattern of human existence, and reconciliation and righteousness before God.

Now one thing cannot be overlooked if this analysis of chapter 5 is taken in the light of the transitional statement between 3:21–4:25 and chapter 5. The opening thought of chapter 5 is "Having been made righteous out of faith."[26] All that proceeds in chapter 5 describes the new existence for the righteous, reconciled, and redeemed person, who has accepted Jesus as his "expiation" (3:25). As chapter 5 unfolds, a difference is noted between the era of Adam and the era of Christ. During the first era, human destiny was determined by Adam's sin of disobedience; but in the second era Christ's obedience did not determine human fate. Rather, individuals must respond to Christ's act in faith in order to be incorporated into the new era.[27] It is hardly necessary for Paul to reiterate this every paragraph, since 5:1 makes it obvious that he is speaking to and describing the destiny of believers.

To describe the faithful person as one who is included in a new era inaugurated by Christ gives rise in Paul's thought to two corollary ideas: the believer's association with Christ and the believer's relation to sin now that an era characterized by grace has been entered. The two are interrelated.

At the beginning of chapter 6 of Romans, Paul realizes that his brief statement about the Law in 5:20 could be misunderstood. If the believer enjoys the removal of the guilt of his sins, and if the believer is assured of salvation at the judgement day on the grounds of the new era established by Christ's resurrection, and if grace abounds more and more wherever sin is present, why be concerned with sin? Let it continue, grow, abound! All the more grace! That his thoughts could be interpreted in this manner is a horror to Paul. He responds with the most emphatic negative he can muster. "By no means!" "Oh, God, may that never happen!"

The believer is no longer interested in sin, and it cannot continue to be the determining factor in existence, because he has died to sin (6:1). "For he who has died is freed from sin" (6:7). "Consider yourselves dead to sin" (6:11). "Let not sin therefore reign . . . Do not yield your members to sin . . . Sin will have no dominion over you" (6:12–14). Just as the dead no longer respond to stimuli of the living neither does the believer respond to the stimuli of sin. It no longer meets with a response in the life of the believer because he or she has died to sin.

This death to sin is balanced, however, by being "alive to God in Christ Jesus" (v. 11). Paul can say this because *believers, in their decision of faith, become so intimately associated with Christ that they share in all that has or will happen to Christ.* Such a concept reflects Paul's Hebrew heritage which could think in terms of corporate unity or corporate personality. This is the idea that a community or a group collectively and individually share together what happens to one another, especially their leader or representative. A passage from the OT will help in understanding this point.

> Then I brought your fathers out of Egypt, and *you* came to the sea; and the Egyptians pursued your fathers with chariots and horsemen to the Red Sea. And when they cried to the LORD, he put darkness between *you* and the Egyptians, and made the sea come upon them and cover them; and *your* eyes saw what I did to Egypt; and *you* lived in the wilderness a long time.
> (Jos. 24:6f.)[28]

By noticing the italicized *you* it is evident that Joshua is associating his audience of at least two generations later with what happened to those Hebrews who crossed the sea. What had happened back there in the past was a part of the corporate expression of the group in the generation to come. Likewise the covenant made by God with Moses at Mt. Sinai continued to bind the people together in every generation. From the Passover ceremony in Jesus' day it was certain that those participating felt a personal sharing in the benefit of that first Passover. "We were slaves to Pharaoh in Egypt, and the Lord our God brought us forth from hence with a strong hand and an outstretched arm." [29] By making such a confession the participant was attesting to the solidarity between himself and his people for countless past generations. Furthermore, under some circumstances one individual could sum up in himself the corporate personality of the entire people of Israel. On the Day of Atonement the high priest, representing the entire nation, could confess all the iniquities of the people and transfer them to the scapegoat which was led away, thus symbolizing the removal of sin for the entire group. Then still representing the people, the priest entered the holy of holies where he was met by God, who accepted the corporate confession and forgave the corporate guilt of the people.[30]

To the Hebrew mind the ability to be joined in the corporate solidarity of the larger group or with representative individuals brought a sense of belonging and destiny that is not always apparent in contemporary Western culture. Yet some similar phenomena do exist to some extent, for it is part of the psycho-social process that the individual identifies to some degree with others. Frequently he projects an ideal image, either a composite or a single hero, from which he takes his lifestyle and life goals.[31] Even in the "individualism" of Western culture, evidence indicates that the individual is capable of and does identify with models outside himself that control his destiny. It is along this line that Paul's thought at this point can be understood. Humans by their natural birth identified with Adam in a lifestyle characterized by sin. But a new era with a new model emerged. Christ ushered in the age of grace. By faith human beings can identify with Christ. What has happened, is happening, and will happen to Christ is experienced by the believer. Events in Christ's life, his attitudes and his destiny, are shared by the believer, for he or she becomes a part of the corporate personality of Christ.[32]

This intimate, profound, association of the believer with Christ is emphatic throughout Paul's writing. The concept is frequently contained in the phrase "in Christ Jesus."[33] He also repeatedly uses verbs with the prefix *syn*, which is usually translated "with" as well as the prepositional phrase "with Christ." These phrases are Paul's effort to refer to the profound reality that the believer was associated with, being made like, sharing a destiny with, and enjoying solidarity with Christ.[34]

In Romans chapter 6, Paul answers the question of whether one will continue in sin by recalling the believer's oneness with Christ:

> Do you not know that all of us who have been baptized into Christ Jesus were baptized into his death? We were buried therefore with him by baptism into death, so that as Christ was raised from the dead by the glory of the Father, we too might walk in newness of life.
>
> (Rom. 6:3f.)

The thought of these two verses, with the exception of the reference to baptism, is implicit in the foregoing chapter.[35] By faith the believer enters into corporate solidarity with Christ, the new model, the bringer of a new era. This includes sharing in the death of Christ.

Since vv. 5-11 are a further exposition of the seed idea in vv. 3 and 4, an understanding of the former will make clear the latter.

Verses 5-11 interpret the death and resurrection experience of Christ and show how the believer shares in it. Verse 5 begins with a premise: "We have been united with him in his death." Greek grammar supports this interpretation as well as the assertion in v. 4 that the believer was buried with Christ in his death. The assurance that comes from this erudition is that the believer will also share in Christ's resurrection.

Verses 9b and 10a describe Christ's death: "death no longer has dominion over him. The death he died he died to sin, once for all." Death is a non-repeatable experience; he died once, and that is all! That event is past. He cannot die again. To say "once for all" is to emphasize the uniqueness of his death. He died once, and never again, to sin. Now that death has occurred sin no longer is a threat to him. But in what way did Christ die to sin? In contrasting Adam and Christ, Paul refers to Christ's act of righteousness (5:18) and his obedience (5:19). This is in relation to God. In comparison to Adam, Christ refused to yield to temptation and sin. He remained obedient to God. He in effect died rather than sin.[36] This was a victory that humanity after the image of Adam could not attain. On the one hand, Adamic humanity gave in to sin and in due course died because of its lack of obedience to God. Christ, on the other hand, accepted the ultimate threat of sin, namely death, rather than be disobedient. His obedience proved victorious. Having died to sin, sin no longer threatens his victory, for he becomes the leader of a new humanity that is superior to Adamic mankind.

Now what does the sharing in the death mean to the believer? Paul can say that he "died for us" (Rom. 5:8), "he became a curse for us" (Gal. 3:13), or "one has died for all, therefore all have died" (2 Cor. 5:14). Paul elaborates further:

> We know that our old self was crucified with him so that the sinful body might be destroyed, and we might no longer be enslaved to sin. For he who has died is freed from sin.
>
> (Rom. 6:6f.)

The meaning of this quotation would be more obvious if the translation began, "We know that the old man was crucified." This is a reference to the Adam type man, a person styled according to the former era. *When the believer is united in a death like Christ's it means his old life style has died, and this brings to an end his "sinful body."* Body is more than flesh and blood. It is a reference to the total person. The total person is sinful in that he or she is oriented according to the style of Adam's example which is disobedience—sin. All of this has been put to death. The believer experiences a death of the former self and the emergence of a new self. So if the Adamic nature within the believer is dead, death no longer holds a threat to him; neither does sin which leads to death. Being dead to sin, it is no longer a guiding factor in one's existence. Because of an intimate association with Christ, the believer shares a corporate solidarity with him. What happened to Christ becomes an experience shared by the believer. Christ died to sin. The believer died to sin!

If the believer shares in the death of Christ, *he also shares in his life*: "We shall certainly be united with him in a resurrection like his" (v. 5b). "We believe that we shall also live with him" (v. 8b). "For we know that Christ being raised from the dead will never die again" (v. 9a). "The life he lives he lives to God" (v. 10b). Paul is thinking of Christ in his resurrected life with God. For Paul, along with the early Christians, it was the resurrection (and ascension) that verified Christ's role as reconciler and bringer of a new era. The resurrection signaled the start of the new era. First Corinthians 15:20-28 is instructive here. Christ, the resurrected one, the first fruits, will, at the full manifestation of the messianic era, make all alive who belong to him. Paul's thought, both in 1 Corinthians and Romans seems to hold in the future the final "aliveness" in Christ. The believer has already died to sin, Christ lives within him now in the present, but in the future the believer will enjoy the same kind of life with God that Christ already enjoys.[37]

In vv. 5b and 8b the tense of the verb is deliberately future. Having identified with Christ in a death to sin, the believer is assured, on the basis of Christ's own resurrection, that he or she will share in a life like Christ's. The believer stands between a past event in the life of Jesus, the cross, which is operative in one's life, and the expectation of a future fulfillment, which will be complete identification with Christ in the heavenly life. Paul's use of the future tense is consistent with this understanding, for he fully elaborates this view in 1 Cor. 15:20-28. Furthermore, this scheme of thinking is present in Rom. 5:1-11, a passage both introductory to chapter 6 and somewhat parallel in thought. Although Paul, as stated before, comprehends the life of the believer as life in the closest possible association with Christ, he carefully guards against saying that believers already possess the ultimate heavenly type existence. But this does not deter the importance or motivational force of the concept of a future heavenly life for the believer. Rather it becomes the hope for living with Christ today. So Paul concludes this paragraph in Rom. 6:11 by exhorting his readers to think of themselves as already "dead to sin and alive to God in Christ Jesus." This will keep them from misunderstanding his doctrine of grace and from questioning whether it is advantageous to continue in sin.

Now what does all of this have to do with baptism? This analysis of Rom. 6:5-11 must inform the understanding of Paul's reference to baptism in vv. 2, 3, and 4 because vv. 5f. explains vv. 2-4. Also it must be remembered that Paul is using baptism to help explain his main idea rather than to explain baptism. Briefly stated Paul's main idea before and after Rom. 6:3f. is *the believer's intimate association with Christ* as the bringer of a new humanity through his death and resurrection.

Paul specifically calls attention to baptism in the matter of Christ's death. "All of us who have been baptized into Christ Jesus were baptized into his death." The "all of us" are those in chapters 5 and 6. *Baptism recalls that the believers are associated with Christ. They share corporately in the event of greatest importance in the history of salvation—his death.* Everything Paul says in chapter 5 and 6:1-11 about the believer sharing in Christ's crucifixion is recalled in the believer's participation in baptism. Paul intensifies the association of baptism with Christ's death by saying "we were buried therefore with him by baptism . . ." (v. 4). He thereby assures the believer of the once and for all nature of dying with Christ; however, he does not follow the expected analogy of Christ's resurrection and the believer's resurrection from the waters of baptism. If this were the symbolism in baptism, Paul fails to capitalize on it. From his further elaboration in vv. 5-11, however, Paul places the complete sharing in Christ's resurrected life in the coming messianic era. It is understandable that he does not draw the comparison in v. 4.[38]

The present blessing of Christ's resurrection must not be overlooked. Instead of saying that the believer is resurrected in v. 4, Paul says that "as Christ was raised from the dead . . . we too might walk in newness of life." This new kind of life is explained in 6:6 and 11 as analyzed above. Because of Jesus' death and resurrection the old Adamic person can die, and the believer does have a new lifestyle in reconciliation to God. This "newness" is the dimension of righteousness that Paul elaborated in chapter 4 and resumed in 5:1. The word "walk" in the phrase is one of

Paul's favorite words to refer to the total style of conduct of the Christian.[39] So there is here a slight reference to appropriate conduct of the Christian. This theme will be dealt with further in chapters 7, 8, and especially 12-14. In the immediate passage Paul wants his readers to realize that association with Christ does include a new style of personal conduct.

Throughout Romans Paul emphasizes the importance of faith as the response to God's reconciling act in Christ. Such a response is worthy of being accounted righteous. His allusion to baptism here in only two verses hardly suggests that baptism assisted or stimulated the faith response. Instead Paul speaks as if his readers know what he means by baptism. From the previous section, and from the analysis of the present context, to recall the event of one's baptism was to recall one's intimate association with Christ, especially in his saving death. If after the personal experience of baptism a reference to baptism recalls this intimate association, then to what else could it have reference as the believer prepared to be baptized? Believers, accepting the presentation of the gospel with its emphasis on Christ's death, gladly entered the baptismal waters to dramatize their faith response to the salvation event in Christ and to indelibly associate themselves with their Lord.

Association with His Death

There is a striking similarity between a statement in Col. 2:12—"and you were buried with him in baptism"—and the baptismal language of Rom. 6:3f.[40] For as the latter, so the former context deals with the importance of being associated with Christ in the salvation event.

Paul addressed a letter to the Christians at Colossae because, somewhat like the young Christians in Galatia, they were incorporating into the gospel he had taught them elements inconsistent with his understanding of God's salvation in Christ. Because of this Paul argues for Christ's supremacy over all creation; Christ brings redemption (1:15-20).[41] Since Christ overcame all threatening spiritual forces (2:15), the Colossian Christians should not be intimidated because they do not observe extraneous regulations (2:16), for Christ freed them from all superstitions (2:20). It is in an effort to develop that argument at a specific point that he refers to baptism.

A new section of the epistle begins in 2:8, and opens with a compact paragraph which applies 1:15-20 to the salvation of the Colossians.

> See to it that no one makes a prey of you by philosophy and empty deceit, according to human tradition, according to the elemental spirits of the universe, and not according to Christ. For in him the whole fulness of deity dwells bodily, and you have come to fulness of life in him, who is the head of all rule and authority. In him also you were circumcised with a circumcision made without hands, by putting off the body of flesh in the circumcision of Christ; and you were buried with him in baptism, in which you were also raised with him through faith in the working of God, who raised him from the dead. And you, who were dead in trespasses and the uncircumcision of your flesh, God made alive together with him, having forgiven us all our trespasses, having canceled the bond which stood against us with its legal demands; this he set aside, nailing it to the cross. He disarmed the principalities and powers and made a public example of them, triumphing over them in him.
>
> (Col. 2:8-15)

In v. 8 the reader is aware that for Paul there in only one source for salvation, namely Christ. Any other source of information or claims is suspect. This assertion is based on the fact that in Christ the totality of deity dwelt.[42] The adverb "bodily" is added to highlight the reality of the presence of the dwelling of the divine in Christ. Paul does not want to run the risk of his readers interpreting the phrase in symbolic fashion. This is Paul's way of emphasizing that Christ was the locale where the Colossians could learn all they needed to know about God and his salvation (v. 9). To make the argument more applicable to his readers, Paul reminds them that they gained a complete and satisfying understanding of their salvation in Christ (v. 10). He appeals to their prior experiences! Did you not find in Christ the fulfillment of all your efforts to discover your proper relation to God? In vv. 9 and 10 the phrase "in him" should be underscored, for it recalls Paul's use of the term "in Christ" to refer to the intimate association of the believer with the Lord. Grammatically the pronoun "him" refers to "Christ" in v. 8. Paul's thought here develops from the idea that Christ is the very embodiment of God's salvation to humanity—the "fulness" dwells "in him." Since the believer is "in him" he shares *that* "fulness."[43] Again the mentality that can think in terms of corporate personality is present here.

Verse 11 further amplifies the significance of Christ by beginning with "in him." This continues the awareness of intimate association and participation in the experiences of Christ, specifically calling attention to the circumcision of Christ. Whether the

Colossians were being led astray by "human tradition" which required physical circumcision or whether they interpreted devotion to particular regulations (2:21) as spiritual circumcision is still debated.[44] Yet one thing is certain: the Colossians understood that Paul was dealing with an important concept in using the term "circumcision." From reading this verse they will recall that they participated in Christ's circumcision. There was no question; this was not a reference to the eighth day surgical process performed upon the newborn infant nor the physical rite of a proselyte entering Judaism; for it was "made without hands." Furthermore, it was not the removal of the foreskin but rather a taking off, or stripping away, the "body of flesh," i.e., the removal of one's natural state of existence. To remove one's this-world-orientation is a concept deeply rooted in Paul's thought that was present in Rom. 6:6 in the picturesque language of crucifying the old man. To "take off" the this-world-orientation is in keeping with Paul's symbolism of "putting on" Christ in Gal. 3:27. So already this paragraph (Col. 2:8–15) is in the same vane of thinking as Paul's other baptismal contexts.[45]

In Rom. 6:6 the crucifying of the old self was designed to remind the believer of participation in the death of Christ. By participating with him the believer is transformed to a new style of existence. To crucify the old self focuses on the same salvation event as putting off the body of the flesh. Both recall the death event of Christ and the believer's association with him. That is why it is appropriate to interpret "the circumcision of Christ" as a reference to his death. In addition, Paul, almost parenthetically, recalls that the believing readers were "buried with him in baptism." This is an abbreviated form of the same thought in Rom. 6:4 and an obvious reference to the death of Christ. Then in v. 12b the thought moves on to the resurrection, and the circumcision of Christ stands in the very place where the death should have been mentioned.

Why has Paul called Christ's death his circumcision? While the specific understanding of circumcision in Colossae may not be determined, it was the symbol with which the Christians were familiar and to which they attached much importance. Paul then can use this familiarity with the term to recall their experience of association with Christ. "If you wish to talk about circumcision, then here is a way to make it meaningful." In addition to the immediate background, the general background of Hebrew circumcision provides insight into the matter at hand. In referring to Abraham, Paul gives a succinct definition of circumcision: He received circumcision as a sign or seal of the righteousness which he had by faith while he was uncircumcised (Rom. 4:11). That is, circumcision was the outward drama that God had established a promise of salvation in Abraham. What was earlier effected in Abraham's relation to God was signaled in the rite. Christ's death as his circumcision, then was the dramatization of the salvation destined in him by God from before the foundations of the earth. That which was established beforehand is now made apparent to all in the event of Christ's death. This was his circumcision.

Christ's resurrection always follows his death in the thinking of Paul, so he turns in v. 12b to stress the believer's association with Christ in that event. For clarity's sake the modern reader must be aware of a grammatical and translational difficulty at the point in v. 12 where the RSV reads "in which you were also raised with him." It would be preferable to translate the phrase: "in him (Christ) you were also raised together." Two considerations support this translation. First, the phrase, "and you were buried with him in baptism," belongs with v. 11 and further amplifies the sharing in Christ's circumcision. The content of vv. 11 and 12a requires this and the grammar certainly permits it. Second, the relative pronoun beginning the second phrase of v. 12 may refer grammatically either to baptism (which) or Christ (him). When the original sentence is diagrammed,[46] the retranslation above, "in him," stands in parallel with "in him" at the beginning of vv. 9 and 11. All three "in him" phrases comprise part of a complex grammatical construction describing Christ, the last word of v. 8. Paul is in effect saying in vv. 9–12 three things about Christ: (1) "in him dwells the fulness"; (2) "in him you were circumcised"; and (3) "in him you were raised."

Returning to the idea that the believer shares in Christ's resurrection, Paul predicates this sharing upon the believer's faith in the powerful action of God in raising Christ. Christ did not just arise from the tomb; rather, God acted, his power was operative. He was the agent effecting Christ's resurrection. So that to which the believer is ultimately responding in faith is the power of God. Was the fulness of deity present in power to effect the resurrection of Christ? Only if it were, could the death-resurrection ever be the salvation event. Only if it were, could Christ be the bearer of salvation. To Paul the answer is plain.

The next reasonable turn in the thought of this paragraph is to the transformation which takes place in the one who responds in faith and participates in Christ's death and resurrection. In v. 13 the person prior to faith is described as dead and uncircumcised, caught in the natural existence of humanity—the Adam type. This holds on to the imagery begun in v. 11 with a reference to circumcision. If circumcision is the putting to death of the old self then uncircumcision is existence according to the old nature. But faith changes all this, and God gives a new self to men and women. The theological concept expressed in this verse is identical with that expressed in Gal. 4:4: "God sent . . . his Son, . . . to redeem those under the law."

In order to give content to the idea of being made alive and for the sake of giving his readers ample opportunity to reflect upon this matter, Paul uses three phrases to amplify the meaning of "God made alive."[47] First, God has forgiven (v. 13). Participating in the death-resurrection of Christ means that the believer is forgiven by God. The estrangement resulting from mankind's rebellion is overcome by God, who, without reservation, restores and makes alive. In the first part of v. 13 the phrase "dead in trespasses" occurs. Humanity is considered guilty of violating whatever laws were appropriate. Having broken them, its style of life is like "death." God, in his power of resurrection demonstrated in Christ, reversed this. Mankind is forgiven, made alive. The second phrase (v. 14) says that God cancelled the bond. The bond is the signed statement verifying the debt of the indebted. When taken along with the preceding statement, this phrase suggests that the one indebted in trespasses has actually certified in writing his indebtedness.[48] Having recognized one's debt, there is a certain legal demand that the debt be satisfied. In this case God cancels the debt, bringing life to the debtor.

The third unit carries this debt cancellation one step further. The certificate of debt is nailed to the cross, for the cross is God's public declaration that he wills to reconcile estranged mankind to himself. God verified his desire to forgive and cancel trespasses. "God has therefore radically transformed our relation to him."[49] This radical transformation that comes about through one's response to God's act in Christ holds cosmic significance. Whatever "principalities and powers" held humanity's spiritual allegiance before are now exposed as invalid attempts to satisfy the human need for reconciliation with God. God's act in Christ at the cross achieved this.

Following this paragraph with its baptismal reference, Paul turns again to warn the Colossians against being intimidated by those who do not agree with his doctrine of salvation (2:16-19). He then begins to apply this theology of transformation to his readers. They are dead to those things which once motivated them—the old way (2:20-23)—but alive to the new life in Christ (3:1-4). The old life which was put to death (3:5-11) is contrasted with the new life which they are to put on (3:12-17). The book continues with an ethical tone. Paul persuasively states his understanding of salvation (2:8-15) and then makes a transition to an application of what this salvation means for conduct.

It can be seen from this analysis of Colossians that Paul's ability to think of corporately sharing in the experiences of Christ underlies the focal passage of 2:8-15. The believer responds in faith and thus participates in the circumcision of Christ, his death, and also his resurrection. Further participation with Christ is present in the living of the new style of life.

Now in the midst of this focal passage, almost incidently as it were, Paul reminds his readers, "you were buried with him in baptism." Grammatically this participle phrase belongs to the previous verse as a further explanation of the believers' sharing in Christ's circumcision.[50] For the readers who may not be understanding precisely the circumcision imagery, the recollection of baptism pinpoints the event in which they shared Christ's circumcision. The sharing in his death is also a sharing in Christ's circumcision.[51] The second half of v. 12 moves on to the idea of resurrection and leaves the baptismal phrase somewhat suspended, for he does not follow through with the baptismal imagery.[52] If the rite of baptism could have provided an analogy of death and resurrection, Paul fails to capitalize on it.[53] Furthermore, Paul turns immediately to the resurrection of Christ and the believers' faith in it as the means of salvation (v. 12).

What then is the function of the reference to baptism at this point? It recalls to mind the believers' participation in the death of Christ. From the context this was Paul's intent. This is as much as can be learned from this reference. Although Paul does not elaborate, baptism does fall in a context in which the significance of the death of Christ is being interpreted (vv. 13b, 14). As in Romans 6, so here baptism was that experience in which the believer shared in the death of Christ and all of its redemptive meaning. It was the event in the life of the believer when the response of faith to God's offer of salvation in Christ was dramatized. The one being baptized willingly associated with the salvation event of Christ, which centered in his death.[54]

Belonging to All

When an individual responds in faith to the redeeming act of God in Christ, he or she not only enters into a new relation to God in Christ but he or she also enters into a community fellowship with all those who have made the same response. The believer's belonging to a community is an integral part of Paul's thought. As a Hebrew Paul was aware of the special place of the people of Israel in the design of God (Rom. 3:2). They were bound not only to God because he chose them through the covenant with Moses but they also were bound to one another because of their confidence in the covenant. They were aware both of their vertical relation to God and their horizontal relation to one another. As a chosen people Israel had a destiny assigned to the corporate community. "You are a kingdom of priests" (Ex. 19:6).

The early Christians were not hesitant to lay claim as rightful corporate heirs to the corporate promises made to Israel. A comparison of Ex. 19:1-6, where God speaks to Moses about the covenant with Israel, may be compared with 1 Pet. 2:9-10, where Peter almost paraphrases the former reference and applies it to the Christians. The early Christian theologians could make this transference of promises from the people Israel to themselves because of their Christology, which recognized that indeed Jesus of Nazareth, crucified and resurrected, was the one true Messiah of Israel. Jesus was a Jew; he fulfilled Jewish Scriptures; he was approved by God. As the Messiah of Israel, he was the one in whom all the ancient hopes and promises were fulfilled and the one who would continue the destiny of the elect people. Believing in the messiahship of Jesus, the early Christians were aware of the rejection of his claim by the Jewish people. For them, this meant that the Jews had forfeited their claim to the promises of God's salvation to the Gentiles by the preaching of the apostles, and in turn a new Israel was constituted.

The idea that gentile believers constitute a new people of God is found in Paul's thought. In Romans where Paul is trying to understand the place of the Jew in God's plan, he quotes Hosea (1:10; 2:23) to verify that God would one day choose those other than Hebrews to be called his people. In speaking to the Philippians he says: "We are the true circumcision" (3:3). "So then you are no longer strangers and sojourners, but you are fellow citizens with the saints and members of the household of God" (Eph. 2:19).

Especially in Romans 11, Paul uses the figure of the grafting of a wild olive shoot on to the old trunk as an effort to convince his Christian readers that they are in the mainstream of God's salvation plan. They are a corporate body in God's design.[55]

One interesting symbol used in the OT to describe the relation of the people to God is the marriage relation. "And in that day says the Lord, you will call me, "my husband!" (Hos. 2:16).[56] In the NT this symbol is applied to the relation between Christ and his body, the church. Ephesians 5:21-33 focuses on this relationship and symbol.[57] In this text the author merges a discussion of the relation of a believing husband to a believing wife with a discussion of the relation between Christ and his body, the church. The OT quotation from Gen. 2:24 and Paul's explanation of it provides the clue to the entire paragraph:

> "For this reason a man shall leave his father and mother and be joined to his wife, and the two shall become one." This is a great mystery and I take it to mean Christ and the church.
>
> (Eph. 5:31f.)

The author is thus giving the basis for his foregoing interpretation. He and interpreters before him recognized the importance of Gen. 2:24 as the divine sanction for marriage. More than that the statement is also a mystery—something that was hidden with God but recently made known.[58] The ultimate meaning of the text is the relation of Christ and his church. That is to say, this one verse can be applied to the marital unit on the one hand and the Christ-church unit on the other.

Beginning with the marital unit, note how the text is applied:

> Even so husbands should love their wives as their own bodies. He who loves his wife loves himself. For no man ever hates his own flesh, but nourishes and cherishes it, as Christ does the church.
>
> (Eph. 5:28f.)

A new personality image has taken shape within the marital unit. Neither act independently of the other. What one does affects the other to the extent that both lose their old individual identity as they work out a shared identity, thus becoming one. Out of a genuine union of husband and wife emerges one new personality that each has shared in creating. If such terms in the verses above as "own bodies," "himself," and "own flesh," are taken as references to the total person, the personality, or better yet, the self, as appropriate to the Pauline view of the person, the suggested interpretation is valid.[59]

To direct the above interpretation to Christ's relation to the church is legitimate since the author holds in parallel this relationship and that of husband-wife. Verse 29 concludes by saying that as a husband has this attitude toward his wife so Christ has a similar relation to the church. The two, Christ and his body the church, are united. Together they form a new unit which takes on a new personality, projects a new image, and has a new destiny. There is a corporate solidarity between them. The new unit, Christ-church, is an organic whole which functions as one. One caution should be observed. This is not a democratic union between two people, each demanding equal rights, etc., for the context makes quite clear otherwise. Without negating what has already been said, Christ, like the husband in the context, has a preeminent role. Christ is the head of the church (v. 23), and is responsible for giving it its life through his own self-giving (v. 25). While Christ and the church function as one, the corporate unit is always aware of what brought it into existence and sustains it. Furthermore, it must be recognized that the author understood "church" and "body" as encompassing the totality of believers. Especially the term "body" exemplifies how an entire community can be summarized in one singular term. The relationship here being described is between Christ and his believers as a corporate unit.

In giving himself for the church it is said that "he might consecrate her by the washing of water with the word" (v. 26). The best understanding of "the word" is "the word of faith which we preach" (Rom. 10:8). "The word" was none other than the gospel of salvation proclaimed by the early Christian preachers. This was the medium which led to the setting aside of the believers as the new people of God, the church. If the "washing of water" is a reference to baptism, it is only vague and illusory and in no way suggests a literal washing which cleanses from sin, for it has already been pointed out that this is contrary to the total biblical tradition.[60]

To summarize Eph. 5:21-33: The author takes the symbol applied to God and his people in the OT and applies it to the relation of Christ and his church. Genesis 2:24 serves as the OT text. This emphasizes the organic unity between Christ and his church and further identifies the church as his body. Both the term church and body must be understood as references to the community of believers.

Turning specifically to the concept of the body as the corporate body of believers, there is a concern for inner unity as it relates to Christ. Paul's first letter to the Corinthians deals extensively with this problem. A reference to baptism appears in the first chapter where Paul is trying to heal the disunity caused by factions, and later in the epistle he refers to baptism again when he deals with disunity arising out of an improper concern for spiritual gifts.

> For just as the body is one and has many members, and all the members of the body, though many, are one body, so it is with Christ. For by one Spirit we were all baptized into one body— Jews or Greeks, slaves or free—and all were made to drink of one Spirit.
>
> (1 Cor. 12:12f.)

The term "body" as a symbol for the organic unity of the church is obvious. The individual believers are like different parts of the body acting in concert. The reason that this phenomenon can take place is because of Christ. "With Christ" all become *one*, are knit together, welded into a unit, acting in unison. How has this been accomplished? By recalling their baptism the answer would be obvious. In baptism each member participated in the same physical process. Each knew that it was the same Spirit in his or her inner being challenging him or her to respond to the gospel in faith. Each knew that through the instrumentality of the Holy Spirit confessing "Jesus is Lord" was possible (1 Cor. 12:3). Thus each was reconciled to God, having come to baptism as a declaration of a willingness to be associated with Christ in an intimate way and to share the very experiences of the Lord. Each believer dramatized a decision for Christ in baptism. This was the basis of unity—each person shared a common inner spiritual experience and outer expression. All had a common faith.

This creates community—common experiences. So Paul stresses this: "We were all baptized into one body." The very fact that all submitted to a baptism which was shared by believers before them attested to their willingness to be associated with them. Baptism then became an occasion to confess one's association with all fellow believers—a declaration of community. The "one body" is the body of Christ. "Now you are the body of Christ and individually members of it" (1 Cor. 12:27).

Paul is here stressing that aspect of baptism that attests to corporate solidarity among believers. He spoke before of baptism as that event that declares one's response to Christ, intimate association with him, and sharing his death and resurrection. Yet even when he refers to baptism in other writings, he does not omit the idea of unity with fellow believers. In the Galatian baptismal reference Paul recalls that "you" (plural) have been baptized and as a result of that baptism you enjoy a unity with one another, for the things that normally divide mankind—race, slavery, gender—are no longer important. Believers are one in Christ. That is to say having been baptized into Christ there is a kinship among believers that negates all divisive considerations and creates a corporate solidarity. So also in 1 Cor. 12:13; those things that divided men and women in the past are now overcome—race, slavery, status. Further, in the Galatians section the baptized are addressed as "sons"—a term signifying a close relation. Much of what was said above about Romans 5 and 6 may be directed toward the idea of community, for the entire thrust of the contrast of the Adam-Christ eras is that Christ inaugurates a new humanity—a new community. Throughout Romans 6 the believers are referred to by the plural pronoun. Paul's thought is obviously for the totality of the group as well as its individual members.

First Corinthians 12:12–13 brings into bold relief this aspect of baptism. The believer by participating in baptism declares a solidarity with all believers who have, likewise, responded to the proclamation of God's salvation in faith and have entered into an intimate association with Christ.

The Book of Ephesians also follows this understanding of baptism. Believers are sons and daughters of God through Christ (1:5). Because of this they have entered into a corporate unity and are the genuine heirs of the promises of God to Israel. Once they were alienated from Israel (2:12), but now in Christ they are fellow citizens and members of the household of God (2:20). Within this community there are no barriers to unity, for Christ is the "peace" which makes all into one by destroying the hostility (2:14).

In a long paragraph (Eph. 4:1–16) the author exhorts the readers to maintain unity and proceeds to identify those items which believers have in common as a basis for unity.

> There is one body and one Spirit, just as you were called to the one hope that belongs to your call, one Lord, one faith, one baptism, one God and Father of us all, who is above all and through all and in all.
>
> (Eph. 4:4ff.)

Unfortunately he does not elaborate upon each item; he assumes the readers understand. He wishes to summarize the common spiritual blessings shared by all believers so that he can move on to a further discussion of the different functions within the body (vv. 11-16). No believer should feel inferior or superior as a result of his or her assigned role, for each is a part of a corporate whole, which functions as an organic unity. Regardless of their respective tasks in the church, every believer shares the same Spirit which spoke to his spirit the things of God and the same hope which grows out of Christ's resurrection. All look forward to the time when they will participate in the final resurrection. They serve the same Lord Jesus Christ, and they actualize the same faith-response to the Lord. They are all baptized as a demonstration of their association with Christ and their fellow believers. They worship the same God who like a Father gives his bountiful salvation to all mankind.

The understanding of baptism along the lines discussed in this chapter may be read into the term "baptism" here in Eph. 4:4ff. and certainly the author would expect each of the other terms— one Lord, one faith, one God and Father—to recall an interwoven complexity of thought in the mind of the readers. Obviously, however, he intended baptism, along with the other items, to witness to and verify the unity which all believers share. How can a single reference to baptism do this? It recalls to the mind of each believer an understanding of a personal baptismal experience and reminds him or her that that understanding is shared by every believer. It reiterates to his spiritual sensitivity that be belongs to a community, that he shares in a corporate solidarity, that he is organically included in the body of Christ.

§

Although the Apostle Paul does not deliberately design a theology of baptism, he does refer to its practice enough for the serious reader to discover his thinking on the subject. Baptism dramatizes that response to the proclamation of the gospel which indelibly associates the believer with Christ, his death, and his church.

6
NOTES

1. R. P. Shedd, *Man in Community* (London: Epworth, 1958), v.; he declares there are "over two thousand extant treatments of either the life or teachings of St. Paul."

2. The greek verb βαπτίζω is used in Rom. 6:3; 1 Cor. 1:13, 14, 15, 16, 17; 10:2; 12:13; 15:29; Gal. 3:27. The noun βάπτισμα, appears in Rom. 6:4; Eph. 4:5; Col. 2:12.

3. C. Masson *L' Épître de Saint Paul aux Colossiens* (Paris: Delachaux & Niestle, S.A. 1950), 98ff.; and F. C. Synge, *Philippians and Colossians* (London: SCM, 1951), 68ff.

4. Ibid.

5. This phrase, although not originally applied to Paul, is suggested by F. Herzog, *Understanding God* (New York: Charles Scribner's Sons, 1966), 74, et al.

6. H. Conzelmann, *An Outline of the Theology of the New Testament*, transl. J. Bowden (London: SCM, 1969), 204.

7. Cf. D. E. H. Whiteley, *The Theology of St. Paul* (Oxford: Basil Blackwell, 1964), 145ff.; and F. J. Leenhardt, *The Epistle to the Romans*, transl. H. Knight (London: Lutterworth, 1961), 102, fn.

8. See above, 13–18.

9. Whiteley, *Theology*, 151f.

10. See above, 58–63.

11. Cf. L. Cerfaux, *The Christian in the Theology of St. Paul*, transl. L. Soiron (London: Geoffrey Chapman, 1967), 315ff., for an elaboration of the Christian's relationship with Christ.

12. See above, 99f., for a discussion of Abraham as an example of faith in Romans 4.

13. R. Schnackenburg, *Baptism in the Thought of St. Paul*, transl. G. R. Beasley-Murray (Oxford: Basil Blackwell, 1964), 23.

14. See above, 63–68.

15. Author's transl.

16. Cf. Rom. 6:6; 2 Cor. 5:17; Gal. 2:20; 6:15; Eph. 2:10, 15; 4:24; Col. 3:9ff. For a complete discussion of this point see H. Ridderbos, *Paul: An Outline of His Theology* (Grand Rapids: Eerdmans, 1975), 223f.

17. Cf. *BAG*, 263, for the meaning of ἐνδύω. An insight into the figurative use of this word is found in Athenaeus, a 3rd century A.D. Greek writer (*Deipnosophiste*, 12.537 [Loeb Classical Library]). Here he related a story from Ephippus about Alexander the Great concerning how he would dress in the holy garments of various deities—Ammon, Artemis, Hermes—claiming to himself their qualities. Paul's thought is far superior. He is in no way suggesting that one should take on the garments or symbols of Christ. Rather believers have become associated with Christ.

18. For the support of this point see A. Grail, "Le Baptême Dans L' Épître Aux Galates (III, 26–IV, 7)," *Revue Biblique* 58 (1951): 515ff.

19. Oepke, *TDNT*, 1:536–40ff.

20. Schnackenburg, *Baptism*, 23.

21. Cf. W. D. Davies, *Paul and Rabbinic Judaism*, (London: S.P.C.K., 1955), 38f.; R. Bultmann, *The Old and New Man in the Letters of Paul*, transl. K. R. Crim (Richmond: John Knox, 1967), 61; C. H. Dodd, *The Epistle of Paul to the Romans*, (London: Hodder & Stoughton, 1954), 79.

22. Davies, *Rabbinic Judaism*, 45f.

23. R. Scroggs, *The Last Adam* (Philadelphia: Fortress, 1966), 78f.

24. Davies, *Rabbinic Judaism*, 39f.

25. Leenhardt, *Epistle to the Romans*, 147.

26. Author's transl.

27. Bultmann, *Old and New*, 68f.

28. Shedd, *Community*, 6, for an elaboration of this text. Davies, *Rabbinic Judaism*, 109, also calls attention to this text. (Italics added for emphasis).

29. Cited from Davies, ibid., 103.

30. Shedd, *Community*, 31f.

31. For a modern discussion of this point cf. L. Gilkey, *Naming the Whirlwind* (Indianapolis: Bobbs-Merrill, 1969), Part 2, ch. 4.

32. Davies, *Rabbinic Judaism*, ch. 5; J. S. Stewart, *A Man in Christ*, (New York: Harper & Brothers, n.d.), ch. 4.

33. Cerfaux, *Christian in Theology of Paul*, 312f., esp. notes 1 and 2 on p. 313 for additional insight into why Paul used certain terms.

34. Schnackenburg, *Baptism*, 170f.

35. Dodd, *Romans*, 87.

36. Ibid., 90.

37. Ibid., 89; Dodd notes that "Paul constantly uses *with Christ* of the future state of Christians, as distinct from their present state *in Christ.*" This supports the present interpretation. Leenhardt, *Epistle to the Romans*, 161, does not make this distinction.

38. Cf. Schnackenburg, *Baptism*, 58, who strongly denies the death-resurrection symbol in Romans 6, esp. in view of v. 6.

39. Rom. 8:4; Gal. 5:16; and lexical study in *BAG*, 654. H. Seesemann, "πατέω, κτλ," *TDNT* (1967), 5:943–45.

40. Schnackenburg, *Baptism*, 70f., makes a detailed comparison of Rom. 6:4ff. and Col. 2:12.

41. See above, 94ff.

42. Masson, *Aux Colossiens*, 124.

43. T. K. Abbott, *A Critical and Exegetical Commentary on the Epistles to the Ephesians and Colossians* (Edinburgh: T. & T. Clark, 1953), 249.

44. Masson, *Aux Colossiens*, 125, n. 4, concludes that there is a circumcision party leading the Christians astray. This viewpoint is denied by W. G. Kümmel, P. Feine, and J. Behm, eds., *Introduction to the New Testament*, transl. A. J. Mattill, Jr. (Nashville: Abingdon, 1965), 239.

45. For a word study of Paul use of "put off" and "put on" cf. A. Oepke, "δύω, κτλ" *TDNT* (1965), 2:318f. The two Greek words ἐκδύω (Gal. 3:27) and ἀπέκδυσις (Col. 2:11) have the same root and become "put on" or "put off" by the different prefix. Paul uses "put on" in the baptismal text of Gal. 3:27; "put off" in the baptismal text here in Col. 2:11. By combining the two texts the interpreter may conclude that baptism was the putting off of the old self and the putting on of Christ. For Paul's other use of ἐνδύω cf. 1 Cor. 15:53, 54; 2 Cor. 5:3; Eph. 4:24; 6:11, 14; Col. 3:10, 12; 1 Thess. 5:8.

46. Schnackenburg, *Baptism*, 67, convincingly diagrams the sentence in this manner.

47. Oepke, *TDNT*, 1:542f., esp. n. 59.

48. Masson, *Aux Colossiens*, 127, n. 7.

49. Ibid., 129.

50. Schnackenburg, *Baptism*, 68.

51. Masson, 126.

52. Schnackenburg, 68f.

53. Ibid., 69.

54. Col. 2:8-15 is quite similar in thought to Rom. 6:1-11; however, there is one significant difference at the point of sharing in Christ's resurrectiori. In Romans Paul stops short of explicitly associating the believer with Christ in his resurrection and uses the future tense "shall live" when referring to the Christian's resurrection. On the other hand Col. 2:12 explicitly states that the Christian participates in Christ's resurrection. Here, Col. 3:1, and Eph. 2:6 are the only references in Pauline literature that speak thus. Masson, 126, n. 5, cannot accept this thought as genuinely Pauline, yet Whiteley, 177, does. If Colossians is not written by Paul, then the problem ceases to exist; however, this may not be the only solution unless one expects an extreme rigidity of expression from Paul. For Paul there are three periods in the life of the believer: (1) the period before faith, (2) the period after faith continuing in the world, and (3) the final period when he is with Christ in the general resurrection. Since the death-resurrection of Christ is really one event, it provides the transforming force from (1) to (2) and guarantees the reality of (3). When Paul contrasts (1) and (2) as death and life he is bordering on the idea of resurrection. This is the case in Rom. 6:8. In Colossians the contrast between death and resurrection to a new life just naturally lends to his explicitly saying that the believer has been raised with Christ (Col. 2:12). Even in Colossians, however, Paul does not distort his three-period scheme of the life of the believer (Col. 3:4), and the above exegesis does not associate (3) with baptism. Certainly Christ's resurrection was essential for salvation and an appropriate assurance and motivation to a new style of life for the Christian in the world. Unless we read Paul with a pre-set requirement of expression, we must permit him flexibility of expression.

55. Shedd, 127.

56. Ibid., 164f., and n. 165 for additional bibliography.

57. If Ephesians is not by the Apostle Paul, this paragraph interprets the apostle and is consistent with his thought, so it is instructive for the present study. Cf. 1 Cor. 6:11 and 2 Cor. 11:2 where Paul likens the church at Corinth to a bride in relation to Christ.

58. E. F. Scott, *The Epistles of Paul to the Colossians, to Philemon, and to the Ephesians* (London: Hodder and Stoughton, 1948), 242.

59. For a full discussion cf. W. D. Stacey, *The Pauline View of Man* (London: Macmillan, 1956), esp. 121-214; and R. Bultmann, *New Testament Theology* (London: SCM Press, 1952), 2:191-227.

60. See above, 24ff.

7 | *Decision to Right Relationship*

So long as Christianity operated within the sphere of Judaism it enjoyed certain advantages. Its first leaders—Peter, James, Paul, Barnabas—were reared in the context of the faith of the OT—its language, thought patterns, ceremonies, and rituals. This meant that they had an appropriate pre-conditioning to receive and understand the teaching of Jesus and the proclamation of his messiahship. As these leaders declared their new gospel to those who were already indoctrinated with Judaism, the new converts were readily assimilated into the Christian community. Thus the people of Jerusalem, their neighbors in Samaria, the Ethiopian eunuch, Cornelius, and many of Paul's converts associated with the synagogues in Galatia and other provinces could embrace the new doctrine and easily move into the fellowship of the other Christians. To some extent their familiarity with the Jewish faith had conditioned them to spontaneously receive the Holy Spirit and baptism as in the case of Cornelius (Acts 10:44-48).[1]

A New Stage

At the same time, as Christianity moved into the larger Graeco-Roman world and appealed to people unfamiliar with the rich heritage of the Jewish faith, it became necessary to educate the new converts into a full appreciation of the implications of the Christian faith, much of which was anchored in Judaism. For an example, Paul spends a great deal of time in his letters to Corinth and Thessalonica dealing with rather elementary moral problems

135

of the kind that anyone familiar with Judaism would have adequately understood. That is to say, that beyond the proclamation of the gospel and the spontaneous response of the individual, *the early Christian leaders discovered the necessity of religiously educating the young converts into a more detailed, comprehensive understanding of the Christian life.*

How early and how detailed this process was is not always clear; however, it is certain that in the second century A.D. some churches had arrived at a minimal amount of instruction that must be given prior to the baptism of the convert. This is learned from a Christian writing from the mid-second century entitled the Didache.[2] In the first part of the work the author rehearses two ways of life: The Way of Light and the Way of Darkness. The Way of Light is described in terms that are taken from the Ten Commandments and Jesus' Sermon on the Mount while the Way of Darkness lists various vices and warns against Satan.

The Didache links this instruction to baptism in that after describing the two ways it continues:

> Now concerning baptism. Baptize as follows, when you have rehearsed the aforesaid teaching: Baptize in the name of the Father and of the Son and of the Holy Spirit, in running water. But if you do not have running water, use whatever is available. And if you cannot do it in cold water, use warm. But if you have neither, pour water on the head three times—in the name of the Father, Son, and Holy Spirit. And prior to baptism, both he who is baptizing and he who is being baptized should fast, along with any others who can. And be sure that the one who is to be baptized fasts for one or two days beforehand.
>
> (Didache 7:1-4)[3]

The obvious meaning of the Didache up to this point is that the new converts must be taught what is appropriate to the Christian life, and this teaching must precede baptism. Furthermore, there is a definite ceremony accompanying baptism for both the baptized and the baptizer. Because the pre-baptism instruction and baptismal ceremony is so obvious in this early Christian document, some interpreters have sought hints or clues that this pattern was emerging in the NT writings.

Further evidence of the church's effort to acclimate properly new converts to its doctrines and life is set forth in *The Apostolic Tradition,* an early church manual dealing with various points of order in the early church such as ordination, prayers, and of course baptism. This manual was compiled by Hippolytus, a church leader in Rome about A.D. 200.[4] According to this manual, new converts are first brought before the assembly of the people where a preliminary examination takes place. If the new convert is approved he must spend the next three years in catechetical classes. During this time he is referred to as a hearer of the Word. Having been faithful for three years, the hearer is then ready for baptism.

When the time draws near for baptism, a final evaluation of the candidates is made. The candidates having been approved begin a series of ceremonies on Thursday culminating in the actual rite of baptism on Sunday morning.

> Then those who are set apart for baptism shall be instructed to bathe and free themselves from impurity and wash themselves on Thursday. If a woman is menstruous, she shall be set aside and baptized on some other day.
>
> They who are to be baptized shall fast on Friday, and on Saturday the bishop shall assemble them and command them to kneel in prayer. And, laying his hand upon them, he shall exorcise all evil spirits to flee away and never to return; when he has done this he shall breathe in their faces, seal their foreheads, ears and noses, and then raise them up. They shall spend all that night in vigil, listening to reading and instruction.
>
> They wno are to be baptized shall bring with them no other vessels than the one each will bring for the eucharist; for it is fitting that he who is counted worthy of baptism should bring his offering at that time.
>
> At cockcrow prayer shall be made over the water. The stream shall flow through the baptismal tank or pour into it from above when there is no scarcity of water; but if there is a scarcity, whether constant or sudden, then use whatever water you can find.
>
> (*The Apostolic Tradition* 20:5-21:2)[5]

The candidate bathed on Thursday and fasted Friday. On Saturday the bishop brought in groups for prayer, and an all-night vigil given to instruction was climaxed by the actual baptism at dawn and concluded by the Eucharist or Lord's Supper. Preparation for the latter is indicated in the text by the reference to the vessels each one brought. In the following paragraphs of the text the baptized not only partake of the bread and wine of the Supper but are also given a mixture of milk and honey to recall the promise now fulfilled of "a land flowing with milk and honey."[6]

In his order for catechumens and their baptism, Hippolytus does not specify on which Sunday of the year baptism takes place. The modern reader might conclude that this could be any Sunday. A great deal of evidence, however, does suggest that the favorite time of Christian baptism was Easter Sunday because that Sunday was identified with the resurrection of Christ which was indelibly associated with the Passover of the OT. Later in his manual Hippolytus advises how this should be celebrated.[7] In referring to the "paschal season" he is definitely identifying Friday, Saturday, and Sunday of Easter. This later discussion of Easter weekend may suggest that the author simply assumed the reader would know that the baptism ceremony described earlier was performed on Easter Sunday, for other Christian writers of this period confirm that Easter was the favorite time for baptism.[8]

The concern of the early Christians to preserve baptism as a dramatic, meaningful symbol within the church community is apparent in the process whereby its originally spontaneous enactment, such as seen in the Book of Acts, among those well-oriented in the Jewish antecedents of the gospel is fortified against misuse by those who lack understanding and determined commitment. There would be no reason for the Christian community to be concerned for the perversion of the spontaneous use of baptism so long as Christianity was closely associated with Judaism, but the very practical problem of assimilating converts from a socio-cultural background that was totally removed from Judaism demanded some type of teaching orientation lest the rite of baptism should lose its meaning as baptized converts regressed to their former life. Paul had such a problem at Corinth (1 Corinthians 6) and the author of 1 John experienced the same difficulty (1 Jn. 3:4–10).

Beyond the NT the early churches experienced the debilitating struggle against heresies within their own ranks. In an effort to strengthen their ranks by being more selective in their membership the early Christians withheld baptism until the convert proved commitment and demonstrated an understanding of the Christian way. The Didache and *Apostolic Tradition* attest that baptism came to have a slightly new place in Christian experience.

In this way the importance of baptism as a viable symbol of the Christian life was protected and strengthened. Non-Christians could not judge that baptism, like so many religious rites of their day, had no significant meaning. Older Christians could not look back to their baptismal experience with doubts and questions, for they had been taught well what it meant and what it required.

The Christians of the Didache and *Apostolic Tradition* were in effect preserving the dramatic nature of baptism and intensifying the expressed testimony by placing it at the end of a spiritually enriching process. This entire effort to preserve the meaning of baptism is furthered by placing the baptismal ceremony on Easter morning, thus the recalling of the salvation-giving, suffering, and resurrection of Christ is made the context of the testimony and the object of belief in the baptismal act.

If the historical records of second and third-century Christianity give evidence of an effort to guard and maintain the significant value of baptism among the Christians, is it possible to discover some effort already within the first-century documents of the NT? Certainly! While the writings of Paul do not deal with a specified procedure in the process from conversion to baptism, they do reflect the serious way he understood the meaning of baptism. So it is in the Johannine writings. There the author, like Paul, enhances the meaning of baptism as he brings it into close association with Jesus' own baptism, the Spirit, and the cross.

Baptism Now Saves

Of all the books of the NT 1 Peter may very well be the one which most dramatically calls attention to the importance of baptism. The author's vivid reference of Jesus' preaching to spirits in prison and the sparing of the eight souls in Noah's ark is concluded with an intense assertion: "Baptism . . . now saves you." In spite of the fact that neither the word baptism nor baptized appear again in the book, *it is possible to understand this declaration as the controlling idea throughout the work.*[9]

The intense thrust of this affirmation is immediately felt in that Peter has emphasized the active, dynamic aspect of baptism by making it the subject of a sentence in which the verb is in the active voice. Baptism is an active, energetic matter. It is conceptualized as an act or experience which saves. Nowhere else in the NT is the word *baptism* used as the subject of an action verb. This peculiar sentence structure sets the tone of the thought and affirmation about baptism.

To Peter's first readers the words were lucid. Baptism was that action commanded by the Lord and practiced by Christians everywhere. It was that moment when they entered into a pool or stream to be immersed in its waters. "To be saved" was the promise of the good news which began with Christ and was subsequently carried abroad by the apostles. It meant being spared the negative judgement which awaited everyone at the end of the ages. "Now" was understandable to the first readers as a reference either to "this present age" as contrast to previous ages before Christ or as an emphasis on the immediate present moment when the author was writing or speaking. This will become more obvious later. Peter is simply asserting that the water ritual known to all Christians has the capability of putting them in such a relationship with God that they will avoid the perils of the ultimate judgement.

Such an open-ended statement could soon be misunderstood, so the author hastens to qualify the manner in which baptism saves. So that his readers will not emphasize the physical, mechanical aspect of the baptismal rite, the author emphasizes that baptism is not effective as a cleansing agent—"not as a removal of dirt from the body" (3:21). The thing that saves the Christian is not an action on his part.[10] The author uses some picturesque words that have meaning to his readers. "Dirt" literally refers to "a greasy, viscose juice" being dark and foul.[11] In this text "body" is translated from the word meaning "flesh," the basic, unredeemed nature of man. "Removal," or putting off, is found elsewhere in the NT writings in reference to putting off, as one does clothing, an evil disposition in preparation for receiving exhortations and teachings, usually about worship.[12] By using terminology already a part of the readers' understanding, Peter makes it certain what idea he is negating. Baptism can in no way be interpreted as a process or act that strips away the unredeemed, filthy nature of the participant. There is no magical, superstitious force in baptism. The author is careful by grammatical construction in v. 21 to negate any idea of baptism as a "putting away." This is his way of clearing the minds of the readers of any possibility of erroneous thought about baptism, and preparing them to hear and understand his positive affirmation.

"Baptism now saves . . . as a declaration of an appropriate awareness toward God through the resurrection of Jesus Christ." The word translated in the RSV "appeal" is better understood as "declaration." *Baptism saves in that it is a kind of declaration.* In order to be sure he is understood the author takes pains with the grammatical structure of the sentence. The word "declaration" is placed in apposition with the word "baptism." This is to make certain the reader connects the two terms. "Declaration . . ." becomes the context or definition of baptism. Furthermore, the word translated "declaration" does not appear anywhere else in the NT, suggesting that the author is deliberately choosing a word that is not so common as to be passed over hurriedly; yet the word does appear, either in noun or verb form, often enough in Greek writings to permit a definition of its meaning. In Dan. 4:17 (Eng. tr.) the original language has been translated into the Greek by the same word used in this passage in 1 Peter. In Daniel the context helps define the word to mean "decision."[13]

The word can also mean a declaration in response to a formal request. An interrogation is made which provides the occasion for a declaration in reference to a specific matter. This use of the word is normal in non-Christian literature of the second century A.D. when a deity is asked for advice. His response is the declaration—the word used in 1 Peter.[14] In juridical texts the word comes to mean "agreement" or "contract." One text reads: "The contract is valid, being written in duplicate in order that each party may have one: and in answer to the formal question they declared to each other their consent."[15] The word in the quotation "declared" represents the word equivalent to "declaration" in the above translation of 1 Peter or the word "appeal" in the RSV. Other references could be quoted to emphasize that Peter has chosen a word which, while not common in the NT writings, has not been worn enough to become ambiguous with theological overtones. Peter is making an effort to define carefully the meaning of baptism without distorting its significance. Baptism does save—it saves because it is a declaration—a decision—a pledge to a contract.

Now the content of the declaration that is being made in baptism is "an appropriate awareness," or in the RSV "a good conscience."[16] The exact meaning of the author's thought depends upon the precise meaning of the word here translated "awareness" or "conscience." The etymological meaning of the word is "knowledge shared with another"[17] or "co-knowledge."[18] This word is used in the ancient language to convey the idea that one is consciously aware of a situation, circumstance, attitude, or factor important to his being. This definition comes out well in 1 Pet. 2:19 where the reader is exhorted to endure pain through or by an "awareness" of God ("mindful of God" in the RSV). Here the idea of conscience will not fit, for conscience immediately emphasizes a sense of moral conduct. It is not through the moral conduct of God that one endures pain but rather because he is aware of God's immediate presence in his life.

Or again in 1 Pet. 3:16 the emphasis is on remaining loyal during times of abuse. The RSV has "Keep your conscience clear," leaving the impression that the author wrote an imperative to his readers. Quite the contrary, the imperative is in v. 14b: "Have no fear. . . ." In v. 16a the author uses a participle, "having the proper awareness," with the answer to the question—"Awareness of what?"—found in the previously mentioned reference to "Christ as Lord."

In the two cases other than 3:21 where 1 Peter uses the word frequently translated by "conscience" (2:19; 3:16), he has been consistent in the thought he wishes to convey. A proper understanding of the word itself and the context of each verse dictates that the word should be rendered by an English word which conveys the meaning of "awareness." This same idea will also fit in 3:21. The stressing of the meaning of the word in the direction of "conscience" in 1 Peter may have come about by the way the term has been translated in Paul's writing; however, Paul's use of the term is more in keeping with the above interpretation of 1 Peter than the popular connotation of "conscience."[19]

The writer carefully chose his words: baptism, the initiatory rite of Christianity, saves. It spares one from the unfavorable circumstance of judgement. It does so because it is the declaration of the individual's appropriate conscious awareness in reference to God. The believer can have this appropriate awareness because of the resurrection of Christ. Baptism saves in that it is the moment when the individual testifies to the fact that he shares something in common with God. The one being baptized testifies to a right attitude and proper relationship toward God. He willingly responds with his declaration to anyone who interrogates him. He has become a "co-knower" with God and other Christians that in the resurrection of Christ there is salvation. The baptized is saved because he recognizes the authenticity and divine origin of the message that in Christ God offers mankind the ultimate revelation of his grace.

Now with his precision Peter guards against both the distortion and over-aggrandizement of baptism. It is not something that cancels out the fleshly, human nature as one would wash oneself from filth. It has no mysterious negating powers. Rather, baptism is conceptualized as an active saving agent. It is not to be relegated to a routine ceremony or taken as an appendage to some other process. It saves. Something happens at the time of the experience. It can be described as a saving experience because it is that moment when the individual dramatically declares that he or she is aware of the presence of the ultimate God in his or her life because of a knowledge of Christ and his resurrection. The baptized one testifies that he or she accepts the authenticity of the Christian proclamation. Baptism becomes the articulation and dramatization of the response of faith. Thus it can be affirmed that baptism saves. In 1 Pet. 3:21 the emphasis falls on baptism as the declaration of the right relation to God through the resurrection of Christ. This is the author's way of maintaining the importance of baptism. He associates it as closely as possible with the individual's experience of salvation without making it the instrument or agent of salvation. Looking at the point of view of the individual, Peter understands that the one being baptized is being saved because he or she recognizes that one's response to Christ's resurrection puts one in the proper relation to God. Baptism articulates this for the convert and dramatizes it for those observing.

A Review of the Action

First Peter 3:21 explicitly emphasizes the author's intense concern for baptism. While it is the only place the word "baptism" is used, it may very well alert the modern reader to the possibility that *here is the key to understanding the entire book*.[20] On the one hand, how could the author be so precise in articulating his concept of baptism if it had not been a planned part of his literary work? On the other hand, how could such an intense statement have been a planned part of his work without coming to the surface elsewhere? The fact that the word "now" appears in 3:21 in connection with baptism adds weight to the idea that there is a concern for baptism elsewhere in the book. If "now" is taken to mean the immediate present of the speaker, and if baptism is important in the "now" of v. 21, it is almost impossible to conceive of some chronological sequence in the writing that would insulate baptism from the remainder of the letter. Rather the whole document becomes more understandable if it is read with the idea that the author's concern for baptism permeates its entire fabric.

The form of 1 Peter is that of an epistle. The opening (1:1-2) and closing (5:12-14) verses verify this. The closing sentences also give the author's purpose and strategy. "I have written briefly to you, exhorting and declaring that this is the true grace of God; stand fast in it" (5:12). His purpose is that his readers will maintain their sound position in the Christian faith. The strategy used was to exhort them in it and declare it to them. In the body of the work he declares the certainty of God's grace in Christ and exhorts his readers to respond in patient obedience to the example of Christ. In so doing they will declare a testimony to their own faith before their non-Christian persecutors. The author's literary design makes the document read more like a sermon (homily) than a letter, and there is no reason to exaggerate this into a problem. Even a written sermon designed to be read at a place removed from the author would require a brief salutation and closing remarks.

The opening section of the epistle (1:3-12) is in the form of a hymn of thanksgiving calling to the attention of the reader the place of God, Jesus Christ, and the Holy Spirit in the revelatory event. This section is probably based on a hymn already in use among the early Christians.[21] It begins by identifying the ultimate source of the new life of the converts—God (vv. 3-5). It was God's mercy that brought about the revelation of salvation in Jesus Christ. The change in their life is identified by the phrase "we have been born anew." This was a favorite way of the early Christians to refer to the radical difference that Christ made in them. Jesus declared to Nicodemus: "You must be born anew" (Jn. 3:3). Both references go back to the idea that the world to come would be like a new beginning, a being born again. This concept is brought out in Jesus' statement in Mt. 19:28 where he points out the blessings of the disciples in the new world—the time of a new beginning, a new birth. Behind the entire thought pattern in Matthew, John, 1 Peter, and elsewhere is the Jewish hope of the future when a judgement would usher in a new era of a new style existence characterized by a new moral nature of total righteousness.[22]

Peter's effort is to describe the radically new state of existence that the Christian now enjoys because of what God has done. By asserting that they have already been born anew—experienced a new beginning of existence—he brings the future era into present experience; yet he maintains the future aspect by assuring them of their hope and coming inheritance. With these words all will recognize again the ultimate source and the different style of their new existence as Christians.

While God is the ultimate source of the new life, this hymn, like other early Christian hymns and confessions, is christocentric (vv. 6-9). The genuineness of their faith will be determined in relation to the revelation from God. The context of the revelation is, of course, Jesus Christ (v. 7). Even though these Christians have not seen Jesus, they love him, and their faith rests firmly on the revelation in him. As a result of this love-faith relationship they have salvation. The author here reviews for his readers the essential place of Christ in the gospel. He is God's revelation, his offer, his challenge to man. No Jesus, no salvation; no faith in the revelation in him, no new life; no hope, no inheritance. Without a genuine faith, i.e., a kind that finds its origin, energizing stimulus, and end in Christ, there is no being born anew into a unique dimension of existence. Hearing, or reading this, the converts to Christianity will recognize afresh that Peter is describing their own feelings and response to their confrontation with the gospel—they love Christ, they believe in him, they are not ashamed of their faith even if it demands suffering.

The third stanza of the hymn recalls the role of the Holy Spirit in the reader's salvation (vv. 10-12). It was the force instrumental in bringing the good news to them. The Holy Spirit was that which inspired or motivated those human beings who preached the salvation message to the converts addressed in this letter-sermon. Whether the "prophets who prophesied" (v. 10) are the OT prophets concerned with God's future redemption—now understood by Christians to be Christ, his death and resurrection—or whether they are the early Christian prophets—who inquired of the OT Scriptures, Jesus' teaching, and his Spirit concerning how they should take the gospel message beyond Judea and Judaism, is difficult to decide.[23] Either way the end result is the same. The prophets were serving the present converts in that their work prepared the way for the message to be delivered to them. This is to remind the readers that they stand in a continuum of God's activity and even at the climax of the sequence, for they enjoy more than the prophets or even the angels (v. 12).

God, Christ, the Holy Spirit, and their activity are now recognized in the plan which brought salvation to these converts. By this recitation Peter deliberately focuses upon the basic elements of salvation at the opening of the homily. He is intentionally stimulating his Christian readers to recognize these basic concepts as the *sine qua non* of their salvation. He is in a brief, terse manner leading them through those experiences which provoked a salvation faith in them. It is God, Christ, and the Holy Spirit who give you a new life. The recognition of Christ's relation to God through the working of the Holy Spirit provokes a genuine faith. That is what *saves!*

Now if this opening section is read with the previously discussed meaning of 1 Pet. 3:21, it helps one understand the scheme of the entire letter. Baptism, as the declaration of an appropriate relation to God in the resurrection of Jesus Christ, *saves!* The content of baptism in 3:21 is the theme in 1:3-12. That which constitutes salvation is openly declared in baptism. Thus the author, desiring to move to a point at which he can specifically emphasize the importance of baptism, begins his homily with those matters that are understood and accepted by his readers as basic to salvation.

Decision for Identity

By referring to the convert's continuity with the past in the first section of the epistle, the author anticipates the next section (1:13-2:10). What went on in the past of God's design, namely prophetic activity, came to fruition in them. Having introduced this idea *the author can use the model of the Exodus from Egypt and the attendant developments in the relationship between ancient Israel and God to give additional understanding to his concept of salvation.* Exodus 19:3-6 is the nucleus of that relationship:

> And Moses went up to God, and the LORD called to him out of the mountain, saying, "Thus you shall say to the house of Jacob, and tell the people of Israel: You have seen what I did to the Egyptians, and how I bore you on eagles' wings and brought you to myself. Now therefore, if you will obey my voice and keep my covenant, you shall be my own possession among all peoples; for all the earth is mine, and you shall be to me a kingdom of priests and a holy nation. These are the words which you shall speak to the children of Israel."
>
> (Ex. 19:3-6)

This text can very readily be analyzed by noting the presuppositions, privileges, and obligations. The covenant presupposes God's ability to make a covenant and his concern for the people. He claims dominion over all the earth and calls to the people's attention what he has already done on their behalf. This brief statement of the covenant sets forth the privileges to be enjoyed by the people. They are a special people to God, a thought implying the reception of blessings. They will enjoy the status of priests, and they will be holy. In turn they are obligated to keep the covenant, to be obedient to God's voice. That is to say, God declares their salvation to them in what he has done and will do for them, but there is inherent in the new relationship the demand for obedience. The people are to be holy. This demand becomes explicit in the recording of the Ten Commandments in Exodus 20. This pattern of a statement of relationship followed by a demand for obedience or holiness is not only found in Ex. 19:5f., the declaration of the covenant, but also in Lev. 11:44f. where the requirement for holiness is related to the Exodus.

> "For I am the LORD who brought
> you up out of the land of Egypt,
> to be your God; you shall
> therefore be holy, for I am holy"
>   This is the law.
>   (Lev. 11:45, 46a)

The identifying mark of God's people is not only what he has done but also their manner of response. It may very well be said that the immediate and primary obligation of those redeemed from Egypt was obedience to God. This is what gave them their distinct identity.

Already in the first section of 1 Peter (1:3-12) the presupposition of the converts' relation to God was set forth. While this may be patterned after the Sinai covenant motif, there can be no doubt that the second section of the homily (1:13-2:10) reflects the salvation-demand of the Exodus milieu.[24] Peter's readers are described as: "obedient children" (1:14), "you shall be holy" (1:16), "lamb without blemish or spot" (1:19), "holy priesthood" (2:5), et al. Then the section ends with a specific paraphrase of Ex. 19:5f. and Hos. 2:23. The author is deliberately describing the new converts' relation to God after the model of ancient Israel.

Like the Sinai covenant, Peter's thought also conveys the demand inherent in the declaration of salvation. A summary is given in 1:22:

> Having purified your souls by your obedience to the truth for a sincere love of the brethren, love one another earnestly from the heart.

Such a statement recalls the summary of The Holiness Code (Leviticus 17-26) as stated in Lev. 19:18. Throughout this second section there are enough exhortations for the readers to understand what the author expects of them. Converts are not to be controlled by passions or ignorance (1:14); rather they should be motivated by reverence (1:17). Their lives are to express love (1:22), while they put away malice and every evil attitude (2:1). They are encouraged as "obedient children" (1:14), "newborn babes" (2:2), "having purified your souls" (1:22), to "grow up to salvation" (2:2b). That is to say, something is expected of those who have been born anew! They do not enter the fellowship without a thorough recognition of what is involved.

Only when one understands thoroughly what is expected of him and how he can appropriately relate to the other party or the total situation is he then able to fulfill his destiny or role. More than anything else, Peter designed this section to move in such a way from presuppositions to obligations and privileges that the unified destiny of the new converts may be understood. He comes to his climactic assertion in 2:9f.:

> But you are a chosen race, a royal priesthood, a holy nation, God's own people, that you may declare the wonderful deeds of him who called you out of darkness into his marvelous light. Once you were no people but now you are God's people; once you had not received mercy but now you have received mercy.

Here as in the model of Ex. 19:3-6 the privileges or blessings are obvious. A nobody became a somebody. People isolated became a community. People in spiritual darkness are now in the light. Those to whom he addresses the homily are herewith declared *Somebody*! They have an identity, they now know who they are, to whom they belong, and how they got that way. These verses summarize all that it means to be born again. Here the presuppositions, obligations, and privileges coalesce to give identity and destiny to these converts. They now know who they are: they are the people of God. They know their destiny: they are to witness to what God has done for them (2:9).

Now what does this section have to do with baptism? It is possible to identify several references in this section as allusions to the ceremony of baptism. The idea of being "born anew" (1:3, 23) has been taken as a reference to baptism.[25] Because of a reference in the *Apostolic Tradition* which describes how the newly baptized are given to drink "milk and honey mixed together . . . by which they who believe are nourished like babes," 1 Pet. 2:2 is taken as an allusion to that practice, thus suggesting that this section is applicable to those about to be or newly baptized.[26] If it is assumed that the entire book of 1 Peter is associated with a baptismal ceremony, it is possible to identify the act of baptism taking place between 1:21 and 1:22, making the phrase "having purified your souls" a specific reference to baptism.[27] Or another approach is to associate 1 Peter not only with baptism but also with the Easter season.[28] If this is done then the allusions to Christ's sufferings are a reference to the Christian Passover-Easter festival. First Peter 1:19 brings together both Jesus' suffering in death and the idea of the Passover by likening him to the paschal lamb.

These allusions certainly help the modern reader identify this section of 1 Peter as a part of a baptismal context once the baptismal nature of the entire book is assumed, but alone they could not totally convince. Adding to these allusions the identification of the problem discussed earlier in this chapter regarding the entrance of non-Jewish oriented converts into the Christian fellowship, the possibility of this section being a pre-baptism lecture or sermon may be enhanced. The entire book is addressed to Gentiles (1:14, 18; 2:9f.; 4:3f.). If they are to be adequately assimilated into the Christian faith, which can only be understood with some knowledge of Judaism, the Gentile converts must be instructed. Furthermore, part of becoming a member of a religious group was to attain a sense of self-identity. This is accomplished in this section. Along with this, the noble moral expectation of Christianity is presented. While detailed rules are lacking, the first readers could not miss the fact that much was expected of them in contrast to their former manner of conduct. That is, the author is definitely concerned in this section that the converts understand what is demanded of them in their appropriate relation to God. This concern is later shared by the authors of the Didache and *The Apostolic Tradition*, where the design of those works clearly relates the teaching situation to the rite of baptism in such a way as to protect baptism from perversion by those who enter it without a true knowledge of their involvement.

First Peter may very well be the first step in that direction, for this present section (1:13–2:10), along with the first part of the book, make it quite certain what is expected of the converts in their relation to God. He then calls upon them in 2:9 to *declare* that relationship. This is exactly what is involved in baptism in 3:21.[29] In 1:13–2:10 the converts recognize again that salvation infiltrates their total conduct; it gives them a sense of obligation and privilege in which they recognize their destiny. This *is* their salvation. As a new person, becoming a part of God's people, they are saved. Baptism saves! It saves as a declaration of one's appropriate awareness of God. Involved in that awareness is a holy obedience. There is no new birth without a moral awareness.

There is no holy obedience without a sense of self-identity. So the author uses a model, the Exodus and covenant, out of the continuum of God's mercy to instruct the Gentile converts in an appropriate awareness of God's mercy toward them. The content of this knowledge saves. *Thus the author is from the beginning sections of his book building toward his climax.* He is drawing a theological line from 1:13–2:10 to 3:21. Here is the instruction that will prevent one from entering baptism ignorant of its full meaning. Here is the catechism that rightfully orients the convert to declare his awareness of God.

But all of this is associated with the role of Christ, without which there was no meaning. The being born anew or being ransomed from one's prior futility to the right relation to God is accomplished by the "blood of Christ" (1:19), i.e., his death and his resurrection (1:21); and in 3:21 one is able to make the proper declaration because of the resurrection of Christ.

Beginning with the undersanding of 1 Pet. 3:21 that baptism is the declaration of one's appropriate relation to God, considering the problem of the proper instruction for Gentile converts, recognizing 1 Pet. 1:3–12 as a statement of the foundations of a proper relation to God, and accepting 1 Pet. 1:13–2:10 as a further identification of what makes for an appropriate relation to God, the design of the epistle begins to unfold.

The author properly recognizes baptism as that crucial moment when the apostolic faith will be preserved or perverted. Knowing full well the attractiveness of a mystical, superstitious rite in his day he was determined to guard the importance of baptism and the apostolic faith. Thus with his mind clearly discerning that what is involved in baptism is what saves, he composes a letter-sermon to set forth his basic theological ideas, knowing full well that his literary work would become an exhortation in conjunction with a baptismal service, or perhaps even a challenge for local leaders to be more diligent in instructing the new converts of their fellowship.

Decision to Obedience

Identified as the people of God who are to declare his wonderful deeds, the new converts need specific exhortation to help them fulfill their destiny in the world of their daily existence. Peter turns to this matter in the third section of his homily (1 Pet. 2:11–3:12). *This section is definitely instructional* and has affinity with other instructional sections of the NT.[30] If the author has found the Exodus-covenant model a viable means of expressing the relationship of the convert to God, he has moved ahead to use instructional material as a way of elaborating that relationship in the same way that the OT did.[31] It was not necessary for Peter to develop new material, for the church had already begun to adapt catechetical material from the synagogue. Much of the material adapted in the instructions of the early Christians apparently goes back through the synagogue to the Holiness Code of Leviticus 17-20.[32] While the present section is not a copying of an already existing manual, it reflects the common instructional material of the early church.

The opening verses (2:11-12) reinforce the idea that the Christians are different from the total population. Just as Lev. 18:1-5 demands conduct from the Hebrews different from the Canaanites, so Peter demands from Christians a lifestyle different from those around them. Those to whom Peter is speaking are genuinely converted in that they abandoned the style of life learned through their natural inheritance, and they adopted a style of life commensurate with their new birth in Christ. Thus when a non-Christian observes this new mode of conduct, even in ridicule, he will recognize some strange source of motivation in the Christian and will ultimately recognize that he or she belongs to the household of God.

One way to make the right impression on the non-Christian population was to accept civic responsibilities (2:13-17). Being a new convert to the holy nation of God did not grant immunity from the requirements of the state or license to determine one's own civil laws. The Christian was to remain a vital part of the "secular" community to demonstrate that he was not an undesirable citizen but rather one who recognized that his Lord was interested in human institutions.

Likewise converted slaves must so order their relation to their masters that they would make a good witness. Even when the master is overbearing the slave must patiently suffer in spite of the fact that his conduct has been circumspect. Christ's suffering is the ultimate example (2:18-25).

While the submission of the wife to the husband was part of the cultural pattern of the day, Peter exhorts the wife to adorn herself inwardly with gentleness and a quiet spirit so that, without speaking a word, her manner would be a winning testimony to the non-believing husband (3:1-6). The converted husband is exhorted to respond to his wife with honor due her because they both are on equal standing in the household of faith. They share the same inheritance (3:7).

This section of instruction in which most of the material is concerned with the individual's relation to society and others, concludes with an admonition to the group as a whole. They are to be unified in outlook, feeling, action, bravery of heart, humility, and forgiveness (3:8-9).[33] All of this is brought together in a quotation from Ps. 34:12-16.

This instructional section flows naturally from the conclusion of the previous section of 1 Peter. The former section (1:13-2:10) concluded with a statement giving identity and destiny to the new converts: ". . . God's own people, that you may declare the wonderful deeds of him. . . ." The following section (2:11-3:12) articulates the ways one measures up to this new identity and destiny. The content of holiness (1:16) and the demand of obedience (1:14) are here prescribed. *It has one final goal: to give evidence to the world at large that God's "great mercy" is a reality as exemplified in the life of the convert* so that others too may be converted (2:12b, 15; 3:2). This brings out one of the primary interests of the author, namely the conversion of the non-Christians.[34]

This is just the point! *Baptism must be taken seriously and its significance be guarded.* The baptized moves about in the community as one who has been born anew into a unique community—a holy nation. Now if the uninstructed baptized convert exemplifies no new style of conduct, the populace at large will have an occasion to speak ill of the entire body and make light of the ceremony of baptism. Society would conclude that baptism did not mean what it claimed. Peter is anxious to remove the opportunity for such a criticism. This is the point of contact Peter shares with the Didache and *The Apostolic Tradition.* They, too, express the manner of life expected of the convert. Beyond 1 Peter, they are more explicit in demanding that new converts undergo a period of trial before entering the baptismal waters.

Peter was determined that candidates for baptism understood the full commitment of their faith and that they could find the motivation for maintaining that commitment. He was fully aware that being identified as a newly born member of a holy nation, producing conduct unique to it would not always be easy, especially if the new convert was the object of reviling, evil comments, and forced to bear unjust suffering. So in this section of instruction Peter introduces the example of Christ who "also suffered for you, leaving you an example" (2:21). Like other NT writers, the author cannot introduce Christ's suffering, for any reason, without expressing Christ's ultimate victory and its effecting salvation for the readers (2:22-25). It is both the example of Christ's victory beyond suffering and his winning salvation for the converts that motivated them to maintain their obedient, holy, manner of life even in the face of suffering.

Thus as he moves towards the climactic section of his homily Peter welds together Christ's act bringing salvation, the new life and conduct of the believer, and the motivation for obedience (3:18-22). All of this is contained in the idea of salvation. Or using another phrase, to be aware of God in Christ is to be conscious of those things involved in salvation: a new birth, a holy nation, obedience, a life as a testimony, suffering.

The Model Decision

Continuing the instructional theme of right conduct, and at the same time shaping the contours of thought for a confluence of ideas, the author proceeds along the line that *a convert must maintain faithfulness and integrity at all costs.* Ideally speaking, doing right should never cause any burden for the convert, but practically Peter knew it would. Even so the convert would be blessed in doing good and any fear of the consequences for doing right is negated by the recognition that Christ is Lord. By maintaining the proper awareness of God, the convert will have no trouble in making an appropriate defense to anyone calling his conduct into question. For Christ is on the one hand the ground of his salvation and at the same time the model of his conduct. These two ideas are given significant emphasis throughout the homily, but now they merge into one grand description of Christ's suffering and victory (3:18-22).

Note what Christ did! He died—an experience of unjustified suffering to death; but through his experience he brought those who were unrighteous to an appropriate relation to God—even the present converts. This is the ground of their salvation. It is also their model. Like Christ they should be willing to suffer for righteousness' sake at the hands of others in order that their lived witness might bring some to God (v. 18).[35] On the one hand, the author calls attention to the crucifixion by stating that Christ was "put to death in the flesh." On the other hand, he emphasizes Christ's continuing presence by referring to his being "alive in the spirit." Both of these references motivate the believers to appropriate conduct and assure them of salvation. Christ's plight did not end in death. He was resurrected and continues to live in the spirit. In using the phrase translated "in the flesh" and "in the spirit" in v. 18, the author is simply specifying the sphere of his dying and living.[36] This is the author's primitive way of calling attention to the reality of his physical death in contrast to his victorious resurrection.[37] The one who remains faithful to his commitment will have the assurance of victory in the example of Christ.

Furthermore the faithful should never be disheartened. There is no unbeliever so antagonistic to the gospel that the convert should hesitate to share with him the hope he has in Christ. Did not Christ take the opportunity to carry the gospel to the spirits which had been imprisoned since the time of Noah?[38] The grammatical construction of vv. 18 and 19 will add to the understanding of what is involved here. The phrase "in which" (vv. 19, RSV) should not be taken to refer to "in the spirit" of v. 18 where "being put to death in the flesh" and "being made alive in the spirit" are obvious contrasts.[39] The first phrase, referring to death, has as its parallel member the coming alive or resurrection. The point of action "in the spirit" is quite different from the time Jesus "preached to the spirits in prison" (v. 19). Grammatically the "in which" (v. 19) may correctly be translated as a temporal conjunction meaning "at which time,"[40] i.e., at the time of his death he went to preach to the spirits in prison. The exact manner of his existence is not noted.

This idea that Jesus spent the interval between his death in Sheol or Hades was a very early part of the Christian belief. It was the natural implication of Judaeo-Christian theology to assume that Christ like all departed ones had descended into Sheol. To say that he died was tantamount to saying he had passed into Sheol.[41] Even Jesus himself alluded to it (Mt. 12:39f.), and Peter's sermon in Acts had quoted: "For thou wilt not abandon my soul to Hades" (Ps. 16:10 quoted in Acts 2:27). In the NT it is only in 1 Peter that the activity of Christ while in Sheol[42] is given. He preached to those present in Sheol who had refused to obey God in the day of Noah.[43] Verse 20 is very careful to identify those to whom Christ preached in order to make the contrast between those who were obedient and those who rebelled. From the OT account disobedient humanity is condemned and punished, but there is a way out for the righteous few.

Accepting Jesus' descent into Sheol as the natural sequence after death, why has Peter described his preaching there? Christ's action is a further example to the convert. He did not hesitate to proclaim his witness wherever he was. Those disobedient in the time of Noah are by far the most evil known to the author. "Every imagination of the thoughts of his heart was only evil continually" (Gen. 6:5). So rebellious were they and corrupt that "the Lord was sorry that he had made man . . ." (Gen. 6:6), and he determined to destroy them. If Christ would, in the time of his abode in Sheol, proclaim the good news to these notoriously evil people, from whom can a faithful convert withhold his witness?

The account of this action of Christ not only heightens his role as model to the Christians, but it also broadens the ground of their salvation. Christ, the revealer from God, the one from the heavenly places, has also entered into the arena of the dead. No area of the universe is closed to him. If it were possible to include in "the spirits in prison" of v. 19 a reference to the "sons of God" (Gen. 6:1-4) who are involved in God's displeasure with man, the meaning of Christ's proclamation in Sheol could be expanded, since according to the interpretation of Gen. 6:1-4 found in 1 Enoch 15:3, 8-12, the giants or Nephilim produced by the union of the heavenly men and earthly women became evil spirits. Later it was necessary for God through his righteous angels to shut some of the evil angels in prison (1 Enoch 6ff., also Jubilees 10:5ff.). Yet in prison these angels continued to influence the activity of the evil spirits in the world.[44] That this interpretation and elaboration was known in early Christian theology is attested by Jude 6:

> And the angels that did not keep their own position but left
> their proper dwelling have been kept by him in eternal chains
> in the nether gloom until the judgment of the great day.

Peter and his readers could very well understand the "spirits in prison" to include both the evil men of Noah's day as well as the fallen angels. Not only does extrabiblical interpretation associate the evil angels with the prelude to the flood but so does Genesis 6. For as soon as the angels had left heaven to choose a wife, God says: "My spirit shall not abide with man forever" (Gen. 6:3). Then the very next paragraph takes up the problem of universal wickedness (Gen. 6:5) and thus the story of Noah and the flood.

The fallen angels, now in prison, were a major cause of evil in the world; and their offspring, the evil spirits, continued to propagate it. Thus to include these as objects of Christ's preaching in prison is to broaden the domain of his effective control. Even the demonic forces are subject to his declaration. His proclamation is a direct challenge to the evil forces of the universe. God has made Christ victorious in every avenue known in heaven, on earth, or under the earth. Even in their place of prison the angels who once could receive some joy because of the work of their demonic offspring have now seen face to face the victor over their forces. For the converts to whom Peter is writing, this meant that they had faith in one whose domain was unlimited. He could invade the stronghold of evil and conquer it. He could unnerve and lay waste the demonic forces of the universe. He was indeed the ground and model of their salvation.

Peter's two avenues of thought, the ground of salvation in Christ and Christ the model of Christian conduct, have merged and proceeded to the story of Noah, which recalls the evil of his generation and the disobedient angels. This story was chosen to enhance the role of Christ. It was also chosen because of the flood and Noah's part and the appropriate use that could be made of "water" in the story.

Noah and his family, consisting of eight people, were saved (v. 20). They were saved from the punishment called down by the evil and perverse generation. They were saved from being swallowed up in the sins of their day. They "were saved through water." The author does not here impart any miraculous instrumentality to the water. Passing through the water to the appointed place was what saved them. The author's design is not to elaborate how water saved Noah, but rather to set the stage for his next assertion.

"They were saved through water which is also a pattern for you. Now baptism saves!"[45] With this clear statement the author has reached the climax of his homily. In his opening section (1:3-12) he carefully explains the foundations of salvation for the new converts. He then moves to an expansion of this using the model of the Exodus-covenant to give a sense of identity and destiny to the new converts (1:13-2:10). At that point he instructs the new converts in the content of holy obedience, introducing Christ as the model for Christian conduct (2:11-3:12). Then he merges two strains of thought, Christ the grounds of salvation and Christ the model of Christian conduct. Next he moves deliberately towards baptism as he continues to enhance the role of Christ (3:13-22). Then in one succinct story (3:18-21) the role of Christ reaches its full measure just at the moment that idea of baptism bursts into the author's thought complex. Baptism summarizes and dramatizes all that he has been saying. Being fully aware of the source of salvation, the one who is the object of faith, the demands to obedience, the challenge of the model for conduct, a convert comes to the moment when he or she is consciously aware that these are the things appropriate to a right relation to God. This is the moment when he or she is baptized, for baptism is "a declaration of an appropriate awareness toward God." That is the convert's salvation!

By understanding the meaning of 1 Pet. 3:21, and by accepting it as the climax of the homily, the larger design of the epistle unfolds to the reader and the importance of baptism to the mind of the author becomes more obvious.

Turning from this climactic assertion of the importance of baptism, Peter continues his concern for appropriate conduct in chapter 4:1-11. He then turns to a brief paragraph which possibly anticipates persecution (4:12-19). Then after a brief admonition to the elders of the church (5:1-5), he gives a final admonition and a closing greeting (5:6-14).

§

Thus the epistle of 1 Peter is the only NT book given completely to a concern for baptism. As the rite finding immediate origins in the ministry of John the Baptist and continuing through the ministry of Jesus, the Jerusalem church, then into the Graeco-Roman world, baptism must be carefully guarded lest it become the point of ridicule rather than the moment of salvation. Peter recognized this. The new converts must be instructed, they must be oriented into a total understanding of the faith. Then, being a part of the household of God, they could share the faith through this lived testimony in face of any difficult circumstance.

7
NOTES

1. See above, 53ff.
2. R. A. Kraft, *Barnabas and the Didache*, vol. 3 of *Apostolic Fathers* (New York: Thomas Nelson & Sons, 1965), 76.
3. Transl. ibid., 163.
4. F. L. Cross, *I Peter: A Paschal Liturgy* (London: A. R. Mowbray & Co., Ltd., 1954), 9.
5. Transl. B. S. Easton, *The Apostolic Tradition of Hippolytus* (Cambridge: At the University Press, 1934), 44f. All translations used herein Easton's.
6. *Apostolic Tradition* 23.2; ibid., 48.
7. *Apostolic Tradition* 29.1-4; ibid., 52f.

8. Cross, *Paschal Liturgy*, 9–11.

9. While 3:21 is the only explicit reference in 1 Peter to baptism, and although most recent literature on 1 Peter recognizes the importance of baptism for interpreting the epistle, modern interpreters have failed to understand this verse as the key to the epistle.

Throughout this chapter the title *Peter* is used as a referent to the author of the First Epistle of Peter and is not intended as a conclusion regarding the identity of the author. This is another literary problem.

A word about the grammar of v. 21 is in order. Nestle's Greek text places a period at the end of v. 20 and contains vv. 21 and 22 in the next period. Bo Reicke, *The Disobedient Spirits and Christian Baptism* (Kobenhavn: Ejnar Munksgaard, 1946), 149–172, accepts Nestle's punctuation and gives extensive examples from both Greek and Latin texts where grammatically an appositional antecedent has been drawn into a relative clause. That is to say, βάπτισμα is in apposition with the previous sentence but has been drawn into the relative clause. Thus ἀντίτυπον is adjectival in reference to βάπτισμα (Reicke, 145). An exact translation is difficult, but apparently the rsv has followed this grammatical analysis. Another possibility would be to extend the period beyond the end of v. 20 and place it after ἀντίτυπον of v. 21. A literal translation would be: "a few . . . were saved through water which even in reference to you (is) a pattern. Baptism now saves, not as . . ."

10. Reicke, *Disobedient Spirits*, 144.

11. *BAG* (1957), 745.

12. E. G. Selwyn, *The First Epistle of St. Peter* (London: Macmillan, 1955), 393f.; and P. Carrington, *The Primitive Christian Catechism* (Cambridge: At the University Press, 1940), 61ff.

13. Reicke, *Disobedient Spirits*, 183; H. Greeven, "ἐρωτάω, κτλ," *TDNT* (1964) 2:688.

14. Reicke, ibid.

15. J. H. Moulton and G. Milligan, *The Vocabulary of the Greek Testament* (London. Hodder and Stoughton, Ltd., 1930), s.v., 231f. Cf. G. C. Richards, "I Pet. iii 21," *JTS* 32 (1931): 77, where ἐπερώτημα is shown to be the promise of commitment of an individual who responds to a question. This is based on Latin authors as well as a second-century interpolation of Acts 8:37.

16. Reicke, *Disobedient Spirits*, 185.

17. *LSJ* (1968), 1704.

18. M&M, ad loc.

19. C. Mauer, "σύνοιδα, συνείδησις," *TDNT* (1971), 7:898–919, agrees substantially with the above interpretation; however, he fails to elaborate the meaning in 1 Pet. 3:21; cf. esp. his summary statements on pp. 904, 906, 917.

20. While numerous authors associate 1 Peter with the rite of baptism, they do not emphasize this verse as a possible beginning point. Cf. Cross, *Paschal Liturgy*, 28f. for a reference to the first author's identifying 1 Peter as a baptismal homily.

21. M.-E. Boismard, "Une Liturgie Baptismale Dans La Prima Petri," *Revue Biblique* 63 (1965): 182–208, makes this point by comparing it with paragraphs in Tit. 3:5–7, 1 Jn. 3:1–9, and Col. 3:1–4. The following discussion of 1 Pet. 1:3–12 has accepted Boismard's basic analysis.

22. F. Büschel, "γίνομαι, γένεσις, κτλ," *TDNT* (1964), 1:688. Josephus, *Antiquities* 11.66 uses the term παλιγγενεσία to describe the new beginning the people of Israel experienced when they returned to Judah from their Babylonian captivity.

23. Selwyn, *St. Peter*, 259-68.

24. Boismard, "Liturgie," 195.

25. Ibid., 195f.; Kümmel, *Introduction*, 295; Cross, *Paschal Liturgy*, 29; et al.

26. *Apostolic Tradition*, 23.2.

27. Cf. Kümmel, *Introduction*, 295.

28. Cross, *Paschal Liturgy*, 23-27.

29. The Greek word translated in 2:9 "declare" is not the same word translated "declare" in 3:21, but in both cases the intent of the author is to encourage the Christian to make known that which has brought new life.

30. Selwyn, *St. Peter*, 420, 259, et al.; Carrington, *Catechism*, 27-29, 31, 41, 43, et al.

31. Lev. 11:45; cf. Boismard, "Liturgie," 192.

32. Selwyn, *St. Peter*, 369-75; Carrington, *Catechism*, 18.

33. Selwyn, ibid., 189.

34. B. Reicke, *The Epistles of James, Peter, and Jude*, AB (New York: Doubleday, 1964), 73.

35. Reicke, *Disobedient Spirits*, 215f. for the possibility of the idea that as Jesus is a sin offering, so also are Christians who die amidst persecution.

36. Ibid., 105.

37. Selwyn, *St. Peter*, 197.

38. Reicke, *Disobedient Spirits*, 130f.; C. E. B. Cranfield, "The Interpretation of I Peter iii. 19 and iv. 6," *Expository Times* 69 (1958): 370.

39. Reicke, ibid., 105.

40. Ibid., 103-15.

41. J. N. D. Kelly, *Early Christian Creeds* (London: Longmans, Green, and Co., 1950), 380.

42. Taking "in prison" to mean Sheol. Reicke, *Disobedient Spirits*, 116f.

43. Cranfield, "Interpretation," 370; Reicke, ibid., ch. 2.

44. Reicke, ibid., 70-90.

45. Author's transl.

Epilogue

Beginning with the religious milieu of first-century Palestine, we have seen the importance of making a decision. John the Baptist demanded a decision and an overt demonstration of that decision. Those who responded to John must dramatize their decision. Jesus did not hesitate to respond to John's preaching by dramatizing his own decision/commitment to the will of God and his kingdom. The Gospel writers use the baptismal context as an occasion to dramatize the relationship between Jesus and God. The earliest Christian sermons, for example Peter's Pentecost sermon, called for baptism as the outward act dramatizing the inner decision. Peter's demand for baptism was in continuity with John the Baptist's baptism in that both dramatized the individual's new relation to God and his kingdom. The significant difference, however, was Peter's relating it to the life, death, and resurrection of Jesus.

The Gospel of John stressed that the object of faith, the point of decision, is that Jesus is the Messiah, the bringer of eternal life from God. While the Fourth Gospel's references to baptism are not fully amplified by the author, enough is given for us to know that baptism dramatizes that the participant has made a decision in favor of Jesus' offer of salvation. Likewise the Apostle Paul has given evidence of his understanding. He has not done this by writing a theology of baptism nor by giving a single lengthy discussion of the subject. Rather he seems to assume that his readers know the significance of baptism; and he, therefore, can refer to it in order to explicate the point he is making. From his references to baptism, we interpreted that baptism dramatizes the believer's response to the gospel—his association with Christ, his resurrection, and his church.

Perhaps it is Peter who has epitomized the significance of baptism when he writes: "Baptism now saves you . . . as a declaration of an appropriate awareness toward God through the resurrection of Jesus Christ." The act of baptism is that moment when the believer publicly dramatizes that he or she has come to know God and has accepted his offer of salvation. This knowledge and salvation has come through none other than Jesus Christ. This satisfies my mysterious curiosity about baptism, why I participated in it, and why I continue to administer it. It gives me a sense of identity and calls me to obedience modeled after our Lord. It places me in continuity with the prophets of old and their urge to demonstrate the inner message of God's salvation. It gives me a kinship with John the Baptist, who required a deliberate decision from those who heard his message. It means that I am following our Lord in his willingness to demonstrate his relation to the Heavenly Father; and, within the same dramatic act that he practiced, I am affirming that it is only through Jesus—his life, death, and resurrection—that I can know God and his salvation. Such an understanding of baptism means that I have a unique relationship with those earliest Christians who dramatized their commitment/decision through this act.

Perhaps this study has helped to bring together the many baptismal texts of the New Testament. It has done that for me. I am convinced that they are bonded together by the common thesis as presented: *The Drama of Decision*. The substance of that decision is faith—faith in Jesus Christ as the bringer of salvation from God. Such an understanding of baptism should inform the candidate, administrant, and congregation in such a way as to make the contemporary practice more meaningful. We may not return to the procedure practiced by *The Apostolic Tradition* or the Didache, but there is every reason to encourage many of our contemporary congregations to upgrade the importance of the baptismal ceremony.

I am sure that this study will not be the final statement on baptism. Others will come and each in its own way will explicate the text, and inform and inspire Christians. For the point of each new study is not to finalize but to keep alive the miracle of salvation which is mysteriously dramatized in baptism.

Amen!

Bibliography

Abbott, T. K. *A Critical and Exegetical Commentary on the Epistles to the Ephesians and to the Colossians.* Edinburgh: T. & T. Clark, 1953.

Abrahams, Israel. *Studies in Pharisaism and the Gospels.* Cambridge: At the University Press, 1917.

Aland, Kurt. *Did the Church Baptize Infants?* Translated by G. R. Beasley-Murray. Philadelphia: The Westminster Press, 1963.

Anthaenaeus. *The Deipnosophiste.* Loeb Classical Library. Translated by Charles Burton Gulick. Cambridge: Harvard University Press, 1963.

Arndt, William F. and F. Wilbur Gingrich. *A Greek-English Lexicon of the New Testament and Other Early Christian Literature.* Chicago: The University of Chicago Press, 1957.

Baptism in the New Testament: A Symposium. Translated by David Askew. London: Geoffrey Chapman, 1964.

Barrett, C. K. *The Gospel According to St. John.* London: S.P.C.K., 1955.

———. *The Holy Spirit and the Gospel Tradition.* London: S.P.C.K., 1947.

Barth, Markus. *Die Taufe—Ein Sakrament?* Zollikon-Zurich: Evangelischer Verlag AG, 1951.

Beare, Francis W. *The Earliest Records of Jesus.* New York: Abingdon Press, 1962.

———. "Sayings of the Risen Jesus in the Gospel Tradition: An Inquiry into Their Origin and Source." *Christian History and Interpretation,* edited by W. R. Farmer et al. Cambridge: At the University Press, 1967.

Beasley-Murray, G. R. *Baptism in the New Testament.* London: Macmillan & Company, Ltd., 1963.

———. *Jesus and the Future.* London: Macmillan & Company, Ltd., 1954.

Belleville, Linda. "'Born of Water and Spirit': John 3:5." *Trinity Journal* 1 (80): 1125–1141.

Bernard, J. H. *A Critical and Exegetical Commentary on the Gospel According to St. John.* Edited by A. H. McNeile. 2 vols. Edinburgh: T. & T. Clark, 1928.

Boismard, M.-E. "Une Liturgie Baptismale Dans La Prima Petri." *Revue Biblique*, 63 (1965): 182-208.

Bonsirven, Joseph. *Épîtres de Saint Jean*. Nouvelle edition. Paris: Beauchesne et Ses Fils, 1954.

———. *Palestinian Judaism in the Time of Jesus Christ*. Translated by William Wolf. New York: Holt, Rinehart, and Winston, 1964.

Bowman, John Wick. *The Intention of Jesus*. Philadelphia: The Westminster Press, 1943.

———. *Which Jesus?* Philadelphia: The Westminister Press, 1970.

Brandon, S. G. F. *Jesus and the Zealots*. New York: Charles Scribner's Sons, 1967.

Brooke, A. E. *A Critical and Exegetical Commentary on the Johannine Epistles*. Edinburgh: T. & T. Clark, 1948.

Brooks, Oscar S. "A Contextual Interpretation of Galatians 3:27." *Studia Biblica 1978*. 3 Vols. Edited by E. A. Livingston. Sheffield: Journal for the Study of the New Testament, 1980. Vol. 3, pp. 47-56.

———. "The Johannine Eucharist." *Journal of Biblical Literature* 82 (1963): 293-300.

———. "I Peter 3:21—The Clue to the Literary Structure of the Epistle." *Novum Testamentum* 16 (1974): 290-305.

Brownlee, W. H. "John the Baptist in the New Light of Ancient Scrolls." *The Scrolls and the New Testament*. Edited by Krister Stendahl. New York: Harper & Brothers Publishers, 1957.

Bruce, F. F. *The Acts of the Apostles*. Chicago: The Inter-Varsity Christian Fellowship, 1952.

Bultmann, Rudolf. *Das Evangelium des Johannes*. Göttingen: Vandenhoeck & Ruprecht, 1950.

———. *New Testament Theology*. 2 vols. Translated by Kendrick Grobel. London: SCM Press, 1952.

———. *The Old and New Man in the Letters of Paul*. Translated by Keith R. Crim. Richmond: John Knox Press, 1967.

Burkitt, F. Crawford. *The Gospel History and Its Transmission*. Edinburgh: T. & T. Clark, 1911.

Buse, S. I. "Baptism in the Acts of the Apostles." *Christian Baptism*. Edited by A. Gilmore. Philadelphia: The Judson Press, 1959.

Cadbury, Henry J. "The Ancient Physiological Notions Underlying John 1:13 and Hebrews X.11." *Expositor* Ninth Series, 2 (1924), 430-39.

Carrington, Philip. *The Primitive Christian Catechism*. Cambridge: At the University Press, 1940.

Cerfaux, Lucien. *The Christian in the Theology of St. Paul*. Translated by Lilian Soiron. London: Geoffrey Chapman, 1967.

Charlesworth, James A., ed. *The Old Testament Pseudepigrapha*. 2 vols. Garden City: Doubleday and Co., 1983, 1985.

Clark, Neville. *An Approach to the Theology of the Sacraments*. Chicago: Alec R. Allenson, Inc., 1956.

Clavier, Henri. "Le Problem du rite et du mythe dans le quatrieme evangile." *Revue D'Histoire et de Philosophie Religieuses* 31 (1951): 275-92.

Conzelmann, Hans. *An Outline of the Theology of the New Testament*. Translated by John Bowden. London: SCM Press, Ltd., 1969.

Cranfield, C. E. B. "The Interpretation of I Peter iii. 19 and iv. 6." *The Expository Times* 69 (1958): 53-63.

Cross, F. L. *I Peter: A Paschal Liturgy.* London: A. R. Mowbray & Co., Ltd., 1954.

Cullmann, Oscar. *Early Christian Worship.* Translated by A. Stewart Todd and James B. Torrance. Chicago: Henry Regnery Company, 1953.

Dahl, N. A. "The Origin of Baptism." *Interpretationes ad Vetus Testamentum Pertinentes Sigmundo Mowinckel.* Oslo: Fabritius & Sonner, 1955.

Danby, Herbert, trans. *The Mishnah.* Oxford: University Press, 1933.

Davies, W. D. *Paul and Rabbinic Judaism.* London: S.P.C.K., 1955.

Deissmann, G. Adolf. *Bible Studies.* Translated by Alexander Grieve. 2nd ed. Edinburg: T. & T. Clark, 1903.

de Vaux, Roland. *Ancient Israel.* Translated by John McHigh. New York: McGraw-Hill Book Company, 1961.

Dodd, C. H. *The Apostolic Preaching and its Developments.* London: Hodder and Stoughton, Ltd., 1936.

_____. *The Epistle of Paul to the Romans.* London: Hodder and Stoughton, Ltd., 1954.

_____. *Historical Tradition in the Fourth Gospel.* Cambridge: At the University Press, 1963.

_____. *The Interpretation of the Fourth Gospel.* Cambridge: At the University Press, 1955.

Dunn, James D. G. *Baptism in the Holy Spirit.* Philadelphia: Westminster Press, 1970.

Dupont, Dom Jaques. *Essais sur la Christologie de Saint Jean.* Bruges: Edition de l'Abbye de Saint-Andre, 1951.

Easton, Burton Scott, transl. *The Apostolic Tradition of Hippolytus.* Cambridge: At the University Press, 1934.

Evans, P. W. "The Baptismal Commission of Matthew XXVIII. 19." *The Baptist Quarterly* 15 (1953-54): 19-28.

Farmer, W. R. "Zealots." *The Interpreters Dictionary of the Bible.* George Arthur Buttrick, ed. Nashville: Abingdon Press, 1962. Vol. IV, pp. 936-939.

Flemington, W. F. *The New Testament Doctrine of Baptism.* London: S.P.C.K., 1948.

Foakes-Jackson, F. J. *The Acts of the Apostles.* London: Hodder and Stoughton, 1931.

Foakes-Jackson, F. J. and Lake, Kirsopp, eds. *The Beginnings of Christianity.* 5 vols. London: The Macmillan and Co., Ltd., 1933.

Fritsch, Charles T. *The Qumran Community.* New York: The Macmillan Company, 1956.

Fuller, Daniel P. "The Resurrection of Jesus and the Historical Method." *The Journal of Bible and Religion* 34 (1966): 18-24.

Gardner, Paul D. "A Note on Colossians 2:11-12." *Westminster Journal of Theology* 1 (83): 172-177.

Gartner, Bertil. *The Temple and the Community in Qumran and the New Testament.* Cambridge: At the University Press, 1965.

Gerhardson, Birger. *Memory and Manuscript.* Copenhagen: Ejnar Munksgaard, 1961.

Gilkey, Langdon. *Naming the Whirland.* Indianapolis: The Bobbs-Merrill Co., 1969.

Gilmore, A. "Jewish Antecedents." *Christian Baptism.* Edited by A. Gilmore. Philadelphia: The Judson Press, 1959.

Goguel, Maurice. *Au Seuil de l'Evangile Jean-Baptiste.* Paris: Payot, 1928.

———. *The Life of Jesus.* Translated by Olive Wyon. New York: The Macmillan Company, 1933.

Grail, Augustine. "Le Bapteme Dans L'Épître Aux Galates (III, 26-IV, 7)." *Revue Biblique* 58 (1951): 503-20.

Haupt, Paul. "Philological Studies, No. 5: Blood and Water." *The American Journal of Philology* 45 (1924): 53-55.

Herzog, Frederick. *Understanding God.* New York: Charles Scribner's Sons, 1966.

Hoskyns, Edwyn Clement. *The Fourth Gospel.* Edited by Francis Noel Davey. London: Faber and Faber Ltd., 1947.

Howard, W. F. *Christianity According to St. John.* London: Duckworth, 1943.

———. "Introduction to the Gospel of St. John," *The Interpreter's Bible,* 12 vols. George Arthur Buttrick, et al., eds. New York: Abingdon-Cokesbury Press, 1952, 8:437-63.

———. "Johannine Sayings of Jesus." *The Expository Times* 46 (1934-35): 486-91.

Hunter, A. M. *Introducing New Testament Theology.* London: SCM Press, Ltd., 1957.

Josephus, The Life and Works of. Translated by William Whiston. Philadelphia: The John C. Winston Company, n.d.

Judge, E. A. "The Early Christians as a Scholastic Community." *The Journal of Religious History* 1 (1960-61): 4-15.

Kelly, John Norman Davidson. *Early Christian Creeds.* London: Longmans, Green and Co., 1950.

Kittel, Gerhard and Friedrich, Gerhard, eds. *Theological Dictionary of the New Testament.* Translated by Geoffrey Bromiley. 10 Vols. Grand Rapids: Wm. B. Eerdmans Co., 1964-76.

Kraeling, Carl H. *John the Baptist.* New York: Charles Scribner's Sons, 1951.

Kraft, Robert A. *Barnabas and the Didache.* Volume 3 of *The Apostolic Fathers.* New York: Thomas Nelson & Sons, 1965.

Kümmel, Werner George; Feine, Paul; and Behm, Johannes; eds. *Introduction to the New Testament.* Translated by A. J. Mattill, Jr. Nashville: Abingdon Press, 1965.

Lampe, Geoffrey William Hugo. *The Seal of the Spirit: A Study of the Doctrine of Baptism and Confirmation in the New Testament and the Fathers.* New York: Longmans, Green and Co., 1951.

La Sainte Bible. Paris: Les Edition du Cerf, 1956.

Leaney, A. R. C., transl. *The Rule of Qumran and Its Meaning.* London: SCM Press, Ltd., 1966.

Leenhardt, Franz J. *Le Baptême Chrétien son Origine, sa Signification.* Neuchatel: Delachaux & Niestle S.A., 1946.

———. *The Epistle to the Romans.* Translated by Harold Knight. London: Lutterworth Press, 1961.

_____. "Jean-Baptiste: sa Predication, son baptême." *Les Cahiers Biblique le foi et Vie* 1 (1936): 20-37.

Liddell, Henry George and Scott, Robert. *A Greek-English Lexicon*, revised by Henry Stewart Jones. Oxford: Clarendon Press, 1968.

Lundberg, Per. *La Typologie Baptismale dans L'Ancienne Église.* Uppsala: A.-B. Lundequistska Bokhandeln, 1942.

Major, H. D. A.; Manson, T. W.; and Wright, C. J. *The Mission and Message of Jesus.* New York: E. P. Dutton and Co., Inc., 1938.

Masson, Charles. *L'Épître de Saint Paul aux Colossiens.* Paris: Delachaux & Niestle, S.A., 1950.

Moore, George Foot. *Judaism.* 3 vols. Cambridge: Harvard University Press, 1950.

Moulton, James Hope and Milligan, George. *The Vocabulary of the Greek Testament.* London: Hodder and Stoughton, Ltd., 1930.

Mowinckel, S. *He That Cometh.* Transl. by G. W. Anderson. Nashville: Abingdon Press, (n.d.).

Odeberg, Hugo. *The Fourth Gospel.* Uppsala Och Stockholm: Almqvist & Wksells Boktryckeri-A. B., 1929.

Reicke, Bo. *The Disobedient Spirits and Christian Baptism.* Kobenhavn: Ejnar Munksgaard, 1946.

_____. *The Epistles of James, Peter, and Jude.* A Volume of *The Anchor Bible.* New York: Doubleday & Company Inc., 1964.

Richards, G. C. "I Peter, iii 21." *Journal of Theological Studies* 32 (1931): 77.

Robinson, W. "Historical Survey of the Church's Treatment of New Converts with Reference to Pre- and Post-Baptismal Instruction." *The Journal of Theological Studies* 42 (1941): 42-53.

Rowley, H. H. "The Baptism of John and the Qumran Sect." *New Testament Essays*, edited by A. J. B. Higgins. Manchester: At the University Press, 1959.

_____. "Jewish Proselyte Baptism and the Baptism of John." *Hebrew Union College Annual* 15 (1940): 313-334.

_____. *The Relevance of Apocalyptic.* London: Lutterworth Press, 1944.

Sauvagnat, Bernard. "Se repentir, être baptisé recevoir l'Esprit: Acts 2, 37ss," *Foi et Vie* 80 (81): 77-89.

Schnackenburg, Rudolf. *Baptism in the Thought of St. Paul.* Transl. by G. R. Beasley-Murray. Oxford: Basil Blackwell, 1964.

Schubert, Kurt. *The Dead Sea Community.* London: Adam & Charles Black, 1959.

Schweizer, Eduard. "Das johanneische Zeugnis vom Herrenmahl." *Evangelische Theologie*, VIII (1953), 341-63.

Scobie, Charles H. H. *John the Baptist.* Philadelphia: Fortress Press, 1964.

Scott, E. F. *The Epistles of Paul to the Colossians, to Philemon, and to the Ephesians.* London: Hodder and Stoughton, 1948.

Scroggs, Robin. *The Last Adam.* Philadelphia: Fortress Press, 1966.

Selwyn, Edward Gordon. *The First Epistle of St. Peter.* London: Macmillan & Co., Ltd., 1955.

Shedd, Russell Philip. *Man in Community.* London: The Epworth Press, 1958.

Stacey, W. David. *The Pauline View of Man*. London: Macmillan & Co., Ltd., 1956.

Stagg, Frank. *The Book of Acts*. Nashville: Broadman Press, 1955.

———. *New Testament Theology*. Nashville: The Broadman Press, 1962.

Stewart, James S. *A Man in Christ*. New York: Harper & Brothers Publishers, n.d.

Strack, Hermann L. and Billerbeck, Paul. *Kommentar zum Neuen Testament aus Talmud und Midrasch*. 5 vols. München: C. H. Becksche Verlagsbuchhandlung, 1922-56.

Synge, F. C. *Philippians and Colossians*. London: SCM Press, Ltd., 1951.

Taylor, Vincent. *The Gospel According to St. Mark*. London: Macmillan & Co., Ltd., 1953.

———. *The Names of Jesus*. London: Macmillan & Co., Ltd., 1954.

Thiering, Barbara E. "Qumran Initiation and New Testament Baptism." *Theological Studies* 27 (81): 615-631.

Thomas, Joseph. *Le Mouvement Baptiste en Palestine et Syrie*. Gembloux: J. Duculot, Editeur, 1935.

Titus, Eric Lane. *The Message of the Fourth Gospel*. New York: Abingdon Press, 1957.

Torrance, T. F. "Proselyte Baptism." *New Testament Studies* 1 (1954/5).

Tripp, David H. "Eperōtēma (I Peter 3:21) a Liturgist's Note," *The Expository Times* 92 (81): 267-270.

Trocmé, Étiene. *Le "'Livre Des Actes" et L'Histoire*. Paris: Presses Universitaires de France, 1957.

Wagner, Gunther. *Pauline Baptism and Pagan Mysteries*. Edinburgh: T. & T. Clark, 1967.

Wedderburn, Alexander J. M. "Hellenistic Christian Tradition in Romans 6," *New Testament Studies* 29 (83): 337-355.

Westcott, Brooke Foss. *The Epistles of St. John*. 2nd ed. Cambridge: Macmillan and Co., 1886.

White, Reginald E. O. *The Biblical Doctrine of Initiation: A Theology of Baptism and Evangelism*. Grand Rapids: Wm. B. Eerdmans Publishing Co., 1960.

Whitely, D. E. H. *The Theology of St. Paul*. Oxford: Basil Blackwell, 1964.

Wright, C. J. *Jesus: The Revelation of God*, Book III of *The Mission and Message of Jesus* by H. D. A. Major, et al. New York: E. P. Dutton and Co., Inc., 1938.

SCRIPTURE REFERENCES

OTHER ANCIENT WRITINGS

INDEX TO MODERN AUTHORS

[Chapter numbers given within parentheses, followed by note number.]

Bowman, J. W.
  (1) 18; (3) 8; (4) 28
Brandon, S. G. F.
  (3) 5
Brooke, A. E.
  (5) 22
Brooks, O. S.
  (5) 37
Brownlee, W. H.
  (1) 15
Bruce, F. F.
  (4) 7, 12
Bultmann, R.
  (5) 27, 29; (6) 21, 27, 59
Büschsel, F.
  (7) 22
Burkitt, F. C.
  (5) 3
Buse, S. I.
  (4) 6, 8, 10, 18
Cadbury, H. J.
  (5) 38
Carrington, P.
  (7) 12, 30
Cerfaux, L.
  (6) 11, 33
Clark, N.
  (5) 41
Clavier, H.
  (5) 17
Conzelmann, H.
  (6) 6
Cranfield, C. E. B.
  (7) 38, 43
Cross, F. L.
  (7) 4, 8, 20, 25, 28
Cullmann, O.
  (5) 20, 33
Dahl, N. A.
  (2) 3, 18
Danby, H.
  (1) 3
Davies, W. D.
  (6) 21, 22, 24, 29, 32
Deissmann, G.
  (4) 23; (5) 9
de Vaux, R.
  (2) 2
Dodd, C. H.
  (3) 16; (4) 2; (5) 13, 15, 29, 35;
    (6) 21, 36, 37

Dupont, D. J.
  (5) 15, 16
Easton, B. S.
  (7) 5, 26
Evans, P. W.
  (4) 35
Farmer, W. R.
  (1) 11
Flemington, W. F.
  (2) 21; (5) 25, 28
Foakes-Jackson, F. J.
  (4) 11
Fritsch, C. T.
  (1) 4
Fuller, D. P.
  (4) 32
Gartner, B.
  (1) 8
Gerhardson, B.
  (4) 34
Gilkey, L.
  (6) 31
Gilmore, A.
  (2) 21; (4) 6
Goguel, M.
  (5) 19, 28
Grail, A.
  (6) 18
Haupt, P.
  (5) 38
Herzog, F.
  (6) 5
Hoskyns, E. C.
  (5) 2, 30, 40
Howard, W. F.
  (5) 16, 33
Hunter, A. M.
  (5) 10
Judge, E. A.
  (4) 34
Kelly, J. N. D.
  (7) 41
Kraeling, C. H.
  (1) 12
Kraft, R. A.
  (7) 2
Lake, K.
  (4) 7
Kümmel, W.
  (6) 44; (7) 25, 27